Cambridge Elements

Elements in Language, Gender and Sexuality
edited by
Helen Sauntson
York St John University

LANGUAGE, GENDER, AND PREGNANCY LOSS

Beth Malory
University College London

Shaftesbury Road, Cambridge CB2 8EA, United Kingdom

One Liberty Plaza, 20th Floor, New York, NY 10006, USA

477 Williamstown Road, Port Melbourne, VIC 3207, Australia

314–321, 3rd Floor, Plot 3, Splendor Forum, Jasola District Centre, New Delhi – 110025, India

103 Penang Road, #05–06/07, Visioncrest Commercial, Singapore 238467

Cambridge University Press is part of Cambridge University Press & Assessment, a department of the University of Cambridge.

We share the University's mission to contribute to society through the pursuit of education, learning and research at the highest international levels of excellence.

www.cambridge.org
Information on this title: www.cambridge.org/9781009633871

DOI: 10.1017/9781009633840

© Beth Malory 2025

This publication is in copyright. Subject to statutory exception and to the provisions of relevant collective licensing agreements, with the exception of the Creative Commons version the link for which is provided below, no reproduction of any part may take place without the written permission of Cambridge University Press & Assessment.

An online version of this work is published at doi.org/10.1017/9781009633840 under a Creative Commons Open Access license CC-BY-NC 4.0 which permits re-use, distribution and reproduction in any medium for non-commercial purposes providing appropriate credit to the original work is given and any changes made are indicated. To view a copy of this license visit https://creativecommons.org/licenses/by-nc/4.0

When citing this work, please include a reference to the DOI 10.1017/9781009633840

First published 2025

A catalogue record for this publication is available from the British Library

ISBN 978-1-009-63387-1 Hardback
ISBN 978-1-009-63389-5 Paperback
ISSN 2634-8772 (online)
ISSN 2634-8764 (print)

Cambridge University Press & Assessment has no responsibility for the persistence or accuracy of URLs for external or third-party internet websites referred to in this publication and does not guarantee that any content on such websites is, or will remain, accurate or appropriate.

For EU product safety concerns, contact us at Calle de José Abascal, 56, 1°, 28003 Madrid, Spain, or email eugpsr@cambridge.org

Language, Gender, and Pregnancy Loss

Elements in Language, Gender and Sexuality

DOI: 10.1017/9781009633840
First published online: October 2025

Beth Malory
University College London
Author for correspondence: Beth Malory, b.malory@ucl.ac.uk

Abstract: This Element explores the gendered dimensions of the ways language used to describe, define, and diagnose pregnancy loss impacts experiences of receiving and delivering healthcare in a UK context. It situates experiences of pregnancy loss language against the backdrop of gender role expectations, ideological tensions around reproductive choice, and medical misogyny; asking how language both reflects and influences contemporary gender norms and understandings of maternal responsibility. To do this, the Element analyses 10 focus group transcripts from metalinguistic discussions with 42 lived experience and healthcare professional participants, and 202 written metalinguistic contributions from the same cohorts. It demonstrates the gendered social and symbolic meanings of diagnostic terminology such as *miscarriage, incompetent cervix*, and *termination* or *abortion* in the context of a wanted pregnancy, as well as clinical discourses, on the experience of pregnancy loss and subsequent recovery and well-being. This title is also available as Open Access on Cambridge Core.

This Element also has a video abstract:
www.cambridge.org/ELGS_Malory_abstract

Keywords: health communication, medical misogyny, pregnancy loss, discourse analysis, language attitudes

© Beth Malory 2025

ISBNs: 9781009633871 (HB), 9781009633895 (PB), 9781009633840 (OC)
ISSNs: 2634-8772 (online), 2634-8764 (print)

Contents

1	Introduction	1
2	Calls for Change	11
3	Data and Method	24
4	Pregnancy Loss Language and Notions of 'Good Motherhood'	30
5	Pregnancy Loss Language and the 'Gender Pain Gap'	51
6	Conclusion	66
	References	70

1 Introduction

'*Miscarriage* to me implies that you did something wrong, that you mis-carried your baby.'
– Lived experience focus group participant, May 2024

This Element explores the gendered dimensions and impacts of the ways in which language is used to describe, define, and diagnose pregnancy loss, and how such language shapes experiences of receiving and delivering care during and after pregnancy loss in a contemporary UK context. It uses thematic and discourse analysis to analyse metalinguistic participant contributions from individuals in two cohorts; one made up of people with recent lived experience of bodily pregnancy loss, and the other comprising healthcare professionals whose work involves regular interactions with people experiencing, or who have previously experienced, pregnancy loss. This Element defines 'pregnancy loss' as the death of a baby at any time during pregnancy, as distinct from its use to refer to a loss occurring before it can be categorised as stillbirth (Gershenson *et al.*, 2021, p.323), as well as from the terms 'reproductive loss', a 'more comprehensive term to include the inability to conceive and the death of a fetus before birth' (Valentine, 2019, p.44) and 'baby loss', which is commonly used to encapsulate both losses during pregnancy and post-birth infant deaths, such as neonatal death and sudden infant death syndrome (Reed, Ellis, and Whitby, 2023, online).

Selecting language to refer to such experiences is a fraught endeavour, since there is significant variation internationally, even just in Anglophone contexts. As will be delineated in Section 2, this reflects differences in definition, such as those between the UK, where stillbirth is defined as the death of a baby in utero after 24 weeks' gestation, and the United States, Canada, and Australia, where the stillbirth threshold is 20 weeks' gestation or a birthweight of at least 400 g (Ellwood and Flenady, 2019, p.422). Since these thresholds correspond to expectations of a baby's ability to survive if born, there has been a historical tendency for them to be reduced as neonatal care has advanced, for example from 28 to 24 weeks' gestation in the UK in 1992, 'to reflect the legal limit of viability in that jurisdiction' (Bamber, 2022, p.345). Such 'viability' thresholds also commonly correspond to upper gestational limits for legal termination of pregnancy; as biolaw experts Halliday *et al.* (2023) note, 'in many jurisdictions the legal bright line [threshold] adopted for that boundary is *viability*, generally understood as the point at which the fetus could survive, without assistance, outside the uterus' (p.539; emphasis original).

Lack of internationally standardised definitions and intersections with reproductive rights debates mean that there has been significant terminological wrangling around pregnancy loss, before sensitivity and patient experience are even considered as a factor. As a result, the impact of language in experiences of pregnancy loss has been largely overlooked; as Section 2 will outline in detail, it has been the topic of disjointed, discretely discipline-specific consideration over the course of several decades, but this consideration has resulted in negligible improvements in patient experiences associated with this language. This Element reports on a qualitative dataset gathered as part of efforts to change this, by leveraging linguistic expertise and interdisciplinary collaboration to understand the impacts of language around experiences of pregnancy loss in a contemporary UK context, in a solutions-focused way. This project's goals were to (1) document the impacts of pregnancy loss language, with a particular focus on terminology, and (2) make evidence-based recommendations for ameliorating the documented negative impacts of such language. The project gathered a metalinguistic dataset concerned with the role terminology and discourses associated with pregnancy loss play in the experience of receiving or delivering healthcare. Analysis of this metalinguistic dataset highlighted the significant gendered dimensions of the negative impacts associated with pregnancy loss terminology and discourses. Such gendered dimensions are the focus of this Element.

As will be outlined in detail in Section 3, this dataset was gathered via 10 focus groups and 202 invited written contributions. All participant contributions, across both the lived experience and healthcare professional cohort, are focused on the role of terminology and discourses in the experience of receiving or delivering healthcare. As such, this Element is able to situate participants' metalinguistic perceptions and experiences of diagnostic language around pregnancy loss against a gendered historical, linguistic, and cultural backdrop of medical misogyny, health inequities, and ideological tensions around reproductive choice, asking how the diagnostic language of pregnancy loss reflects and even shapes contemporary gender relations and understandings of pregnancy, motherhood, maternal responsibility, and reproductive choice.

Both lived experience and healthcare professional participants emphasised the impact that diagnostic lexis can have on the experience of pregnancy loss and subsequent recovery and well-being. Many highlighted that in the context of a wanted pregnancy, terminology such as *miscarriage, incompetent cervix*, and *termination* or *abortion* implies that the female body has failed or is to blame, or is associated with stigma around reproductive rights. Often, participants posit a causal link between such terminological implications of guilt or stigma, and their own internalised sense of self-blame or responsibility, or perceived failure to effectively fulfil societal expectations of 'good motherhood' (Hays, 1996; Wolf, 2010; Matley, 2020; Kinloch and Jaworska, 2021).

The metalinguistic reflections around these issues raise two theoretical linguistic questions: firstly, whether such a causal link between language and perception can exist in the way many participants suggest; and secondly, whether eliminating overtly challenging terminology like *miscarriage* and *incompetent cervix* would merely scratch the surface, leaving the misogynistic discourses which led to fossilisation of such terminology in the pregnancy loss lexicon untouched. These issues will be explored in the following subsections, before Subsection 1.5 outlines the structure of the Element.

1.1 A Causal Link?

Language and gender research has been preoccupied with questions of cause and effect for decades, since feminist critiques of language and arguments for non-sexist language reform have raised questions about the extent to which language can be said to determine our worldview. In Deborah Cameron's (2023) words, 'do biases in language just reflect pre-existing societal prejudices, or do they actively influence our perceptions, thoughts and actions without us being aware of it?' (p.14). The poles of this opposition in feminist linguistics are often represented by the strongly determinist Dale Spender (1998) and the anti-determinist Robin Lakoff (1973). For Spender, language is 'man-made', a male invention, and men have had a 'monopoly on naming', even where it relates to bodily experiences like pregnancy:

> Men may know something of motherhood – after all they comprise the majority of obstetricians – but they know only from their specific position as men, and only from the perspective of a spectator. This must provide a limited view of the event, for the meanings of motherhood which men have provided are based on the way in which motherhood relates to them. It would not be at all surprising if motherhood meant something entirely different to those who were the participants. (1998, p.58)

By contrast, Lakoff's anti-deterministic position is that 'social change creates language change, not the reverse; or, at best, language change influences changes in attitudes slowly and indirectly, and these changes in attitudes will not be reflected in social change unless society is receptive already' (1973, p.76). These opposing viewpoints represent an approach to the theoretical questions raised by the so-called 'Sapir-Whorf' hypothesis, seen through a feminist lens. This hypothesis consists of two tenets; firstly, linguistic relativity, or the idea that structural differences between languages correspond to native speakers' cognition; and secondly, linguistic determinism, the idea that language determines worldview. According to this hypothesis, cognition reflects pre-existing linguistic categories and is determined by them.

Whilst in a 'pure' form, the Sapir-Whorf hypothesis has now largely been rejected by linguists and cognitive scientists, a 'weaker form of linguistic relativity has been widely accepted in linguistics' (Graumann, 2007, p.134). This school of thought 'suggests that recurrent patterns of language use may predispose speakers to view the world in particular ways, but that such a worldview is not all-determining' (Ehrlich, 2003, p.13) and thus that, since culture and language are 'two sides of a coin', cultural milieu shapes language, and language also shapes an individual's perceptions of their environment and their role within it (Graumann, 2007, p.134). Crucially, this more nuanced Sapir-Whorfian theory is not deterministic. Whilst the original hypothesis 'means that a speaker's language sets up a series of lexical and grammatical categories which act as a kind of grid through which s/he perceives the external world, and which constrain the way in which s/he categorizes and conceptualizes different phenomena' (Pütz and Verspoor, 2000, p.ix), the weaker form 'not only encompass[es] the idea that language is biased by culture, but also that speakers of a language society have the possibility to conceptualize empirical things and events differently, and accordingly verbalize them in distinct ways' (Graumann, 2007, p.134).

Acceptance of this weaker Sapir-Whorf hypothesis underlies the theories of cognitive semantics and is now uncontroversial. In relation to language and gender research specifically, Susan Ehrlich contends that the 'feminist critique of language allows for the denaturalising of the somewhat invisible and commonsensical assumptions embedded in sexist language' (Ehrlich, 2009, online). As Cameron (1998) notes, therefore, 'to the extent that our lives are carried on in language (which is to a considerable extent, for most of us), the sexism of language must constantly re-enact and reinforce the commonsense 'normality' of sexist assumptions' (p.11). This is the logic underlying anti-sexist linguistic reform attempts in 'cases where bias has been "fossilized" in a particular linguistic form or set of forms, such as the pronoun *he* used generically, the titles *Miss* and *Mrs* (which make a marital status-based distinction the equivalent male title *Mr* does not), or formulaic expressions like "the best man for the job"' (Cameron, 2023, pp.15–16).

The endeavour of this Element, to highlight the sexist biases encoded in pregnancy loss terminology and discourses with a view to linguistic reform, thus sits firmly within a tradition of feminist language critique aimed at questioning such embedded sexism in language. This tradition has questioned 'direct', 'overt' or 'word-based codified' sexism, those 'cases where bias has been "fossilized" in a particular linguistic form or set of forms' (Cameron, 2023, p.15) and often sought reform. As Cameron notes, however, attempts at linguistic reform in such contexts have seen mixed results, since 'replacing one [lexical] form with another may eliminate overt or surface bias' but not the discourses which accompany, and ultimately gave rise to, individual words (Cameron, 2023, p.16). This issue, in relation to the specific context of pregnancy loss language, will be explored in the next subsections.

1.2 Beyond Words?

The results of anti-sexist linguistic prescriptivism have been mixed, and there now exists a body of literature which indicates why this is. As Cameron (2023) notes, attempts at language reform are most likely to succeed if

> (a) its social and political goals command widespread support in the relevant linguistic community, and (b) if it is given linguistic legitimacy by the gatekeepers people regard as authorities on 'correct' or 'acceptable' usage. (pp.169–170)

It thus seems to be the case, as Cameron notes, that such 'attempts to change language don't usually succeed unless the beliefs they embody or affirm have already achieved a certain level of acceptance in the community', meaning that '[t]he discourse [has] to change before the linguistic reform could be successful' (Cameron, 2023, pp.171–172). Understanding the discursive context of the diagnostic terminology around pregnancy loss is thus imperative, if successful linguistic reforms are to be implemented, since there is a risk that 'replacing one [lexical] form with another may eliminate overt or surface bias' but not the discourses which accompany, and ultimately gave rise to, individual words (Cameron, 2023, p.16). This Element thus aims to tackle both the individual lexical units perceived to be associated with gendered difficulties by participants and wider discursive representations around pregnancy loss which relate to gender. It is not possible to separate these concerns completely, but as Subsection 1.5 outlines, the structure of the Element reflects the need to consider them discretely. Thus, Section 4 is more concerned with specific lexical units identified as problematic by participants, whilst Section 5 considers gendered discourses around pregnancy loss in greater detail.

Informed by previous research both on anti-sexist language reform attempts and Feminist Critical Discourse Analysis (Lazar, 2005), the research reported here aims to integrate consideration of the diagnostic lexis of pregnancy loss with consideration of the broader discourses and cultural narratives which are the focus of other linguistic work in this domain (cf. Austin *et al.*, 2021; Horstman, Holman, and McBride, 2020; Littlemore and Turner, 2020; see Section 2). Such linguistic work has demonstrated how problematic these discourses and narrative frames are, but it is possible that without careful consideration of terminology, they will persist. This is because, whilst we know that 'discourse ha[s] to change before [a] linguistic reform [can] be successful' (Cameron, 2023, p.172), in this instance it appears from participant data presented here that some discourses around pregnancy loss have either already changed or are in the process of changing. As a result, for example, the fossilisation of culpability into words such as *miscarriage* and *incompetent* seems to be perpetuating or re-imposing a sense of failure that may otherwise not be felt. The time thus seems ripe to resist the fossilised misogyny of much of the terminology used around pregnancy loss, as well as the discourses that surround these words and phrases. The following subsection will outline how this Element attempts to integrate micro-level metalinguistic analysis with that of macro-level discursive construction.

1.3 Discourses of (Good) Motherhood

In exploring both metalinguistic attitudes to pregnancy loss terminology and the discourses that accompany such terminology, this Element builds on a body of feminist poststructuralist research on gendered parenthood which has sought to critique the impacts of 'dominant' discourses which work to maintain the 'status quo' (Weedon, 1997, p.34). Like this body of feminist discourse analysis (Sunderland, 2000, 2004; Lazar, 2005, 2007), the research reported here is underpinned by a notion of discourse with roots in Critical Discourse Analysis (CDA; Fairclough, 1988; Sunderland, 2004) and the Foucauldian definition of discourse as a form of social practice which 'systematically form-[s] the object[s] of which they speak' (Foucault, 1972, p.49). This means that discourses are not only 'ways of seeing the world' (Sunderland, 2000, p.254) but that also potentially 'determine, or at least shape, our conceptions of an object' (Coffey-Glover, 2020, p.44). Feminist discourse analysis is concerned with gender as 'an idea (or set of ideas) about men/women, boys/girls and gender relations' (Sunderland, 2012, p.29). Its methodology aims to 'trace' this set of ideas, gendered discourses, via systematic investigation of lexico-grammatical choices (Sunderland, 2004).

By integrating consideration of diagnostic lexis for pregnancy loss with investigation of the linguistic 'traces' of gendered discourses (Sunderland, 2004) in lived-body experiences of pregnancy loss, this study thus attempts to integrate micro-level metalinguistic analysis with macro-level discursive construction. In doing so, this Element builds upon a body of Feminist Critical Discourse Analysis (FCDA) research concerned with 'demystifying the interrelationships of gender, power and ideology in discourse' (Lazar, 2005, p.5) and focusing specifically on motherhood. This work has highlighted and sought to challenge what Coffey-Glover (2020) calls 'discourses of normative motherhood', which function to perpetuate constructions of 'good' and 'bad' motherhood.

FCDA scholars such as Mackenzie (2018, 2023), Coffey-Glover (2020), Matley (2020), and Kinloch and Jaworska (2021) have drawn on feminist theory around motherhood to trace the 'repeated acts' of language which underlie the 'rigid, regulatory frames' (Butler, 1990, p.33), or ideas about gender, which police performances (Lazar, 2007, p.151) of acceptable or 'ideal' motherhood. Hays' (1996) theory of 'intensive mothering', a form of hegemonic mothering praxis which necessitates self-sacrifice, underpins much of this research. Wolf (2007) labels this set of social expectations 'total motherhood', defining this concept as 'a moral code in which mothers are exhorted to optimize every dimension of children's lives' (p.615). Crucially, in the context of this Element, Wolf (2007) emphasises that 'total motherhood' can be understood as 'beginning with the womb' (p.615). FCDA scholars have traced both the 'moral' obligation articulated here and the discourse of 'child-centred' mothering in their work. In her work on discourses of exclusive pumping of breastmilk for infant feeding, for example, Coffey-Glover (2020) highlights that feeding with breastmilk allows 'women [to] feel they have fulfilled their moral duties to their child' (p.7). Mackenzie (2019), meanwhile, highlights the dominance of discourses of 'child-centric motherhood' within the Mumsnet Talk thread she examines.

Critical feminist approaches to discourses of motherhood have highlighted not only the 'discursive pressure' (Knaak, 2006, p.413) to conform to the 'moral duty' of 'intensive', 'total', or 'child-centric' motherhood, but also the risks of 'maternal deviance' (Murphy, 1999), or failure to conform to these social expectations. In particular, such failure has been explored in relation to infant feeding, and the framing of formula feeding as 'risky' and therefore 'deviant' (Murphy, 2000; Wolf, 2010; Brookes, Harvey, and Mullany, 2016; Coffey-Glover, 2020), by comparison with breastfeeding. In their analysis of lived-body experiences in Mumsnet life-writing, Kinloch and Jaworska (2021) also highlight that Postnatal Depression 'is experienced as a threat to women's self concept of motherhood' (p.2), and as a failure to fulfil the 'moral' obligations of 'good' motherhood. They also note that, in the context of the Cartesian mind/body dualism prevalent in modern western medicine, which 'has 'dissected' human beings into two separate entities – mind and body' (p.2), physiological aetiologies of Postnatal Depression can be '"desirable" because of their potential to depersonalise and consequently destigmatise postnatal mental illness by distancing the self from the "faulty" body' (p.2). This dualism is reflected in previous studies considering how language is used by people with lived-body experience of pregnancy loss. Littlemore and Turner (2019), for example, report that during the 'Death before Birth' project which explored how those with such lived-body experiences used figurative language to discuss their loss, participants sometimes used 'divided-self' metaphors (p.7). According to Littlemore and Turner (2020), such metaphors 'personified' their body, and 'distanced [it] from the "self"', in order that 'it could be "blamed" for the pregnancy loss' (p.54).

Littlemore and Turner's findings (2019) also indicate that the identity of 'parent', and particularly of 'mother', plays an important role in the experience of pregnancy loss. They note that '[w]hile the bereaved have often begun to form their identities as parents, pregnancy loss deprives them of a means to enact their parental identity' (p.2). This recalls Wolf's (2007) notion of 'total motherhood' as a 'moral code' in which women are expected to perform the role of mother 'beginning in the womb' (p.615). In addition to the social expectation that motherhood be enacted during pregnancy, other scholars have highlighted pronatalist ideologies which portray procreation as 'compulsory' (Ellece, 2012), potentially increasing pressure to safeguard a gestating baby in order to conform to 'good' motherhood. For Ellece (2012), 'compulsory motherhood' is an ideology which suggests that women should naturally desire motherhood and find it fulfilling, and that not feeling this way is unnatural. Moore and Abetz (2019) likewise emphasise that motherhood is associated in their dataset with this kind of 'linear pronatalist narrative of life fulfilment' (p.402). Likewise, Matley (2020) notes that in a Western cultural context, 'ideologies of motherhood as the "ultimate fulfilment" of women remain powerful', despite being 'arguably not as entrenched' as in other parts of the world (p.2).

It is against this backdrop of social expectations of 'good' motherhood, which is 'intensive' (Hays, 1996), 'total' (Wolf, 2007), 'child-centric' (Mackenzie, 2018), and self-sacrificing from its gestational beginning, and which is a 'compulsory' part of being a woman (Ellece, 2012), that pregnancy loss is experienced. It is thus crucial that this Element considers both the causal link some participants posit between terminological implications of guilt or stigma, *and* internalised feelings of self-blame or responsibility which may be linked to normative discourses of 'good motherhood' (Hays, 1996; Wolf, 2010; Matley, 2020; Kinloch and Jaworska, 2021). Section 1.4 will briefly delineate the language used in this Element to refer to processes of pregnancy loss and gender, before Section 1.5 outlines the structure of the Element.

1.4 Note on Language

This Element strives to use language inclusively. In relation to pregnancy loss, this means reflecting the recommendations of this study's quantitative sister project (Malory and Nuttall, 2024) for pregnancy loss terminology in mass communication contexts. It is necessary to acknowledge here, however, that this reflects consensus preference in the UK at the point of data collection in 2024, and that words like *pregnancy loss*, *baby*, and *parent* in contexts of loss will not feel right for everyone.

Gender-inclusive language is also used wherever possible, in an additive manner. In pregnancy-specific contexts, this usually means use of the phrase *women and birthing people*. In contexts of the gender pain gap (Patrick-Smith and Bull, 2024), both *women* and *misogyny-affected individuals* are used, depending on the evidence being reported and whether it relates specifically to cisgender women, as much of the research reported here does, or whether it was designed more inclusively. Where I have not been constrained by the need to reflect the research designs of others, I use *misogyny-affected individuals* to acknowledge that cis women, trans women, non-binary people, and trans men can all be affected by the gender pain gap.

1.5 Structure of the Element

This Element explores the broad question: How does diagnostic terminology for pregnancy loss affect people with lived experience in gendered ways? In order to consider this question, the Element firstly presents background information on the issue of pregnancy loss terminology, in Section 2. Here, previous calls for, and attempts to implement, linguistic reform or standardisation of diagnostic terminology for pregnancy loss are presented and evaluated, and other relevant research in health communication is also presented. Whilst Section 2 considers a reasonably large body of evidence from a variety of disciplinary perspectives, including articles in medical, health communication, sociology, and philosophy journals, newspapers, and magazines, it ultimately shows that such calls for standardisation and attempts at reform have been to be fragmented and lacking in linguistic expertise, systematicity and empirical basis. Section 3 presents an approach which constitutes a radical departure from the literature outlined in Section 2, by presenting the study design used in this Element. Here, the co-production model used to gather data on the metalinguistic perceptions and linguistic experiences around pregnancy loss of lived experience and professional participants is outlined. Demographic information about the lived experience cohort is provided, and the procedures for the thematic and discourse analysis of participant data are delineated.

In Section 4, original metalinguistic data is used firstly to demonstrate the perceived impacts of pregnancy loss terminology in a contemporary UK context. These data show that many lexical items experienced as challenging by lived experience participants reflect gender role expectations and imply failure to conform to maternal stereotypes. Thematic and discourse analysis of lived experience data shows patterns in the metalinguistic perceptions of such lexis. One such pattern, explored in Subsection 4.1, relates to language such as *miscarriage, pregnancy failure, missed miscarriage,* and *incompetent cervix* being experienced as external accusations of culpability and even being perceived as prompting self-blame. Another, related, pattern, explored in Subsection 4.2, relates to the perception that some lexis used around pregnancy loss is associated with stigma, including *termination* and *abortion*. Data explored in this section demonstrate that these words, which are used in contexts of loss as well as where unwanted pregnancies are ended voluntarily, also pose issues relating to gender norms and cultural stereotypes of the good mother and are avoided by some people with lived experience of pregnancy loss due to the perceived stigma they carry. Section 4 highlights the causal relationship many participants posit between lexis and cognition, exploring the role of language in the experience of losing a baby during pregnancy for study participants.

Section 5 shifts the focus of the Element away from the narrow emphasis on cognitive effects of specific lexis in Section 4 and considers the discursive construction of pregnancy loss experiences more broadly. Continuing to present original data extracts, this section highlights the role of terminology and discourses in perpetuating a healthcare environment which systematically dismisses, sidelines, and undermines the pain reported by women and other misogyny-affected individuals in contexts of pregnancy loss, reflecting the wider 'gender pain gap' known to affect such groups.

Finally, in Section 6, the implications of the analysis for policy, clinical practice, and theory are explored. The Element concludes by considering how communication guidance and linguistic reforms that are tailor-made for pregnancy loss contexts might be implemented successfully. This section will consider the findings presented in the Element in the context of questions about socially responsible prescriptivism and diagnostic lexis reform. It will also outline potential avenues for future research on this topic.

This Element and the detailed case study evidence it contains will highlight the serious challenges that pregnancy loss terminology poses for many people, and how clearly many aspects of usage in this context relate to gendered expectations and misogyny. Its goal is to explore metalinguistic perceptions of diagnostic terminology for pregnancy loss, and wider discourses around pregnancy loss, in terms of the gendered experience of accessing healthcare, and to question what role linguistic reform can play in challenging systemic inequities in medical experiences.

2 Calls for Change

This section provides background on previous calls for, and attempts to implement, linguistic reform or standardisation in the diagnostic terminology for pregnancy loss. Each of the following subsections focuses on a different type of call for change, for example those by clinicians in Subsection 2.1, and those in the public domain in Subsection 2.2. By showing that such calls for standardisation and attempts at reform have been fragmented and lacking in linguistic expertise, systematicity, and empirical basis, this section contextualises the study design outlined in the following section, as well as the data and the findings of the analysis delineated in Sections 4 and 5.

2.1 Clinical Calls and Initiatives for Linguistic Reform

There is a long, if somewhat sporadic, tradition of clinical interest in the impact of medical terminology in experiences of pregnancy loss in the UK. For the most part, there is little discernible evidence of direct effect from clinicians' interventions to promote or proscribe specific lexical items, but there is one notable exception to this tendency. In 1985, three eminent experts in recurrent pregnancy loss wrote a letter to *The Lancet* (Beard, Mowbray, and Pinker, 1985), in which they called for *miscarriage* to be adopted as mainstream clinical terminology for referring to spontaneous pregnancy loss before 28 weeks' gestation (after which loss was then classified as 'stillbirth'). They made this plea for paradigmatic substitution based on their observation of the distress that the predominant terminology for referring to pre-28-week losses in the UK, *spontaneous abortion*, caused to patients at their recurrent pregnancy loss clinics. In fact, their strongly worded letter called for use of the word *miscarriage* in such contexts 'on humanitarian grounds', citing the distress *abortion* caused to patients who, they note, 'always speak of 'miscarriages' unless they have had a termination of pregnancy' (pp.1122–1123).

Whilst there is clearly little doubt that in the years following the letter to *The Lancet*, *miscarriage* did supersede *abortion* as the dominant way of referring to spontaneous pregnancy loss before the stillbirth threshold, the reasons for this have been debated. Given the historical context in which the letter was written, less than two decades after the 1967 decriminalisation of pregnancy termination in Great Britain, the need to distinguish between spontaneous and induced pregnancy loss was a fairly novel one. As Moscrop (2013, p.100) highlights, until this point, 'the distinction between "abortion" and "miscarriage" was impossible in clinical practice and meaningless in clinical language', since 'criminal interference' was likely to be suspected in most contexts involving bleeding during pregnancy. Moreover, it has been argued that the shift towards *miscarriage* in clinical usage represented a natural change in usage, reflecting the 'legal, technical, professional and social developments' in the late twentieth century (Moscrop, 2013, p.101), as opposed to a prescriptive effect of the *Lancet* letter. Other analysts did ascribe this linguistic shift to Beard, Mowbray, and Pinker (1985), however; in a 1992 study of usage in the *British Journal of Obstetrics and Gynaecology*, Chalmers (1992) demonstrated an apparent 'change in terminology before and after' (p.357) the letter's publication, whilst Chamberlain (1997) referred to the lexical 'substitution' as being 'catalysed by Beard *et al.*' (p.1684).

The question of whether the change was the result of prescriptive intervention or of the societal pejoration of *abortion* is not one of merely academic interest. As indicated earlier, this case study constitutes a rare exemplar of successful, widespread clinical language reform for the benefit of people affected, and therefore highlights that such reforms can be successfully implemented. In recent years, corpus and computational methodologies have laid to rest question marks over the role of the *Lancet* letter in this linguistic change, showing that it is highly probable that Beard, Mowbray, and Pinker were indeed responsible for catalysing the shift away from *abortion* and towards *miscarriage* (Malory, 2022). The remarkable success of this intervention, prompting as it did a near-wholesale shift from *abortion* to *miscarriage* to refer to spontaneous loss in British clinical usage, is clear when we consider usage of *(spontaneous) abortion* in other Anglophone contexts. In the United States, for example, as recently as 2011, clinicians were still calling for a parallel shift from *abortion* to *miscarriage* in American clinical English (Silver *et al.*, 2011). Considering why Beard, Mowbray, and Pinker were successful, when subsequent clinical calls for language reform have not been, is thus vital in understanding the mechanisms by which the terminology of pregnancy loss can be changed, when deemed problematic.

Silver *et al.*'s (2011) call for *miscarriage* to replace *abortion* in contexts of spontaneous loss reflects the continued tendency for *abortion* to be used in this sense to this day. Whereas the shift in UK clinical usage seems to have been almost complete by the mid-1990s (Malory, 2022), analysis of US obstetrics and gynaecology journals in the late 1990s showed that *abortion* remained the dominant variant (Hutchon, 1998). Whilst the shift in UK clinical usage appears to represent a success for well-being-focused linguistic reform, therefore, Silver *et al.*'s (2011) calls for change highlight not only its geographical but also paradigmatic limitations. As well as *miscarriage*, Silver *et al.* (2011) also call for substitution of *blighted ovum, chemical pregnancy, cervical incompetence,* and *insufficiency*. Whilst clinical usage in the UK had banished *abortion* for spontaneous loss almost totally by the year 2000 (Malory, 2022), the same cannot be said for these diagnostic labels. In these cases, the objections Silver *et al.* (2011) highlighted were just as applicable in a UK context as in a US context. *Blighted ovum* is a phrase used to diagnose loss when a gestational sac is visible on ultrasound and can be observed to grow over a period of weeks, but the baby has stopped developing too early to be seen. Silver *et al.* (2011) object to the phrase on the grounds that it firstly 'makes no biological sense', since it implies a fault with the ovum (egg) and thereby also 'conveys a sense of the loss being due to some inherent abnormality with the mother' (p.1407), a theory which is increasingly discredited. As Agg (2023) notes, 'the idea that this kind of miscarriage is a failure to launch – a failing rooted in the woman's body thanks to a "rotten" egg – is not based in biological reality' (p.196). Silver *et al.* (2011) also contend that the phrase *chemical pregnancy* 'implies that it was not a "real" pregnancy' and that this causes 'anger and sometimes frustration on the part of parents' (p.1403) and highlight 'cervical incompetence' and 'cervical insufficiency' as diagnostic labels which 'place "blame" on the mother'; suggesting 'spontaneous cervical ripening' as a substitute (p.1407). As the findings presented in Sections 4 and 5 highlight, these are all issues lived experience participants in this study grappled with, despite their geographical and temporal distance from the context in which Silver *et al.* (2011) made these objections.

Silver *et al.* (2011) establish a model for the systematic highlighting of problematic diagnostic labels by clinicians in medical journals or associated media, which has since been replicated several times. For example, in a *British Medical Journal (BMJ)* blog in 2018 entitled 'Humanising Birth: Does the Language We Use Matter?' the authors identify 'examples of poor communication' and suggest 'alternative language' (Mobbs, Williams, and Weeks, 2018). Examples relating to loss specifically include 'compassionate induction' for 'terminate pregnancy' in cases of Termination for Medical Reasons, and 'medically complex' for 'poor obstetric history' or 'high risk' (Mobbs, Williams, and Weeks, 2018). Likewise, in a 2021 *Lancet* comment piece, Vimalesvaran *et al.* 'call[ed] out inappropriate, insensitive, and outdated words and phrases that have been historically used in clinical practice, particularly in the intrapartum period' (pp.859-860). Via a table of 'sensitive' and 'insensitive language' (Vimalesvaran, Ireland, and Khashu, 2021, p.860), they suggest 'incompetent cervix' be replaced with 'cervical insufficiency that can increase risk of preterm birth or pregnancy loss', and 'appeal to colleagues worldwide to banish such terms from their vocabulary' (p.860). In a US context, Pinar *et al.* (2018) argue that '[s]tandardized terminology is available, though not universally used' (p.191), and provide a 'Glossary of revised terms for pregnancy loss' (p.194), which is presented as an updated version of Silver *et al.*'s (2011). This glossary distinguishes between 'Proposed nomenclature', such as 'Early pregnancy loss' and 'Old nomenclature', such as 'Spontaneous abortion' (p.194).

There is thus evidence that the 'humanitarian grounds' motivating Beard, Mowbray and Pinker to seek linguistic reform in 1985 continue to rouse some clinicians to linguistic prescription and proscription. However, linguistic prescriptions by clinicians pose a number of issues. Firstly, they seem to have limited success; there is no indication that any such attempt at linguistic reform other than that of Beard, Mowbray, and Pinker (1985) has resulted in significant change in usage. The replication of Silver *et al.*'s (2011) recommendations in Pinar *et al.* (2018) highlights this apparent failure. More concerningly, such prescriptions are often made without an evidence base or any linguistic expertise. As such, they do not reflect contemporary usage or variation in usage, societal attitudes, the preferences of individuals with lived experience, or large-scale research. This can lead to prescriptions that other experts find problematic, or that go against empirical research; for example, as noted earlier, Mobbs, Williams, and Weeks (2018) recommend 'compassionate induction' for *Termination for Medical Reasons (TFMR)*, but this substitution is opposed by leading UK TFMR charity Antenatal Results and Choices, on the grounds that it fails to capture the diversity of experiences of TFMR and could perpetuate stigma.[1] Moreover, recent quantitative research (Malory and Nuttall, 2024) has found comparatively low levels of dissatisfaction with the phrase *Termination for Medical Reasons*, indicating that Mobbs, Williams, and Weeks' (2018) concern is misplaced. This is probably the result of a small number of clinical interactions with individuals for whom the phrase *Termination for Medical Reasons* does pose issues, and therefore highlights the importance of systematic empirical research exploring experiences of, and attitudes towards, terminology and discourses of pregnancy loss; both qualitative, as in the study reported here, and quantitative, as in Malory and Nuttall (2024), as well as research which evaluates the impact of previous attempts at linguistic reform (e.g., Moscrop, 2013; Malory, 2022). This proscription of *Termination for Medical Reasons* also clearly underscores the need for multidisciplinary consultation, and the involvement of non-clinical co-producers affected by pregnancy loss, in this kind of research; since, as the next subsection will explore, calls for linguistic reform around pregnancy loss are also common in the public domain.

2.2 Public Domain Calls and Initiatives for Linguistic Reform

The previous subsection considered clinicians' calls for linguistic reform of diagnostic terminology for pregnancy loss, in contexts including medical

---

[1] Private correspondence with Jane Fisher, Director of Antenatal Results and Choices, 2023.

journals and medical journal blogs. This subsection will demonstrate that this linguistic 'complaint tradition' (Milroy and Milroy, 2012), as well as the model of presenting proscribed terminology alongside prescribed alternatives, also manifests in non-medical genres such as newspapers, magazines, and non-medical blogs, often by 'lay' writers. In only a minority of cases, such complaints about pregnancy loss terminology in the public domain are written by clinicians. One example of a medical professional writing on this topic for a popular audience is a Canadian news article entitled 'It's Time to Stop Calling Pregnancy Loss "Miscarriage"' (Gorfinkel, 2015). In this piece, Canadian GP Iris Gorfinkel argues that the patients she sees who are going through pregnancy loss 'largely continue to be under the false impression that the loss had been self-generated'. Questioning whether the word 'miscarriage' could be partly to blame, Gorfinkel (2015) suggests 'natural pregnancy loss' as an alternative which 'reflects a basic understanding of what pregnancy loss truly represents'.

Gorfinkel's (2015) sentiments were reflected in an article in the US edition of the magazine *Glamour* published online in January 2020 (Oré, 2020). This, too, questioned whether the word *miscarriage* should continue to be used, specifically in the context of the so-called 'wave of conversation on social media' which followed the death of Chrissy Teigen and John Legend's son, Jack. Interspersed with screenshots from Twitter in which users complain about *miscarriage*, the article highlights social media users' linkage of self-blame and the word *miscarriage*, citing 'pregnancy loss' as a preferable alternative. The screenshots from Twitter used in Oré's (2020) piece highlight a popular groundswell of feeling concerning the language used to describe experiences of pregnancy loss, which has led journalist Jennie Agg in her book *Life, Almost* to characterise Teigen's post as 'a relief valve' (Agg, 2023, p.18). This groundswell may reflect a gradual cultural movement away from *miscarriage* and towards *pregnancy loss*, which appears to be manifesting in policy and public health messaging, as will be outlined in the next subsection. Prior to Teigen and Legend's loss, an Instagram post by former *Dawson's Creek* actor James Van Der Beek had gone viral, after he argued that 'we need a new word' to replace *miscarriage*. For Van Der Beek, '"Mis-carriage", in an insidious way, suggests fault for the mother – as if she dropped something, or failed to "carry"' (quoted in Agg, 2023, p.142). Despite such complaints about *miscarriage* seeming to garner widespread support and agreement, however, any change in usage away from *miscarriage* is gradual and piecemeal; totally unlike the swift change towards *miscarriage* in clinical usage following Beard, Mowbray, and Pinker's (1985) call for change.

Elsewhere in the public domain, a more expansive approach to attempting linguistic reform has been taken. The Peanut app, a commercial entity designed to facilitate friendships between parents, has compiled and published a 'glossary' online, entitled *Renaming Revolution: The Motherhood and Fertility Glossary*. Hosted on Peanut's website, this glossary was developed with the avowed intention of kick-starting a 'renaming revolution', which tackles the 'reality that existing terminology does not value and empower women' through pregnancy and birth (Peanut, 2023, p.1). This document was compiled through crowdsourcing on social media, with thousands of women reported to have contributed 'hurtful terms they experienced' (Agatowski, 2023). For pregnancy loss, the document suggests substitutions such as 'early cervical dilation' instead of 'incompetent cervix' (Peanut, 2023, p.3), 'early pregnancy without an embryo' instead of 'blighted ovum', and 'compassionate induction' instead of 'medical termination' (p.6).

The Peanut glossary was compiled with input from a small group of medical professionals and those with some linguistic training but does not rely on an empirical model and fails to take account of all necessary considerations in making recommendations. As noted earlier, for example, *compassionate induction* is considered an inappropriate substitute for *termination* in contexts of Termination for Medical Reasons, since not all such experiences involve delivery via induction. Moreover, Malory and Nuttall (2024) have highlighted reasonably high levels of approval for the phrase Termination for Medical Reasons amongst a cohort of participants who had experienced this procedure. The other examples from Peanut's *Glossary* quoted earlier pose similar difficulties; clinicians involved in the research reported here argue that 'early cervical dilation' is non-specific and does not adequately reflect the particular circumstances encompassed by the admittedly problematic phrase *incompetent cervix*. Likewise, 'early pregnancy without an embryo' could be considered to imply the lack of a baby, which many participants in this study found very distressing. Such suggested substitutions speak clearly to the need for an empirical methodology informed by interdisciplinary knowledge exchange, as is used in the research reported in this Element, if linguistic reform for pregnancy loss language is to be attempted. Prior to the research reported here, the closest approximation of such a framework was the 'consensus statement' model, which will be discussed in the next subsection.

2.3 Consensus Statements and Official Guidelines

It will be clear from the previous two subsections that pregnancy loss terminology poses challenges and is, to some degree, in flux. As such, the previous subsection ended by emphasising the need for both interdisciplinary collaboration and an evidence base for any recommendations relating to language in this domain. There has been very little empirical research on the use and impact of pregnancy loss language prior to this study, but the body of relevant empirical literature that exists will be considered in the next subsection. There has, however, been an increase in interdisciplinary collaboration over the past decade, with so-called 'consensus statements' on diagnostic terminology for pregnancy loss now being produced with input from experts outside the medical profession.

Such consensus statements are designed to provide clarity and consistency of terminology, and are produced using a 'consensus model', following consultation between experts. They therefore provide a systematic overview of perceived problems with diagnostic terminology used in relation to pregnancy loss in English, as well as recommendations for terminology considered (by those involved in their creation) preferable. It is important to stress that these are not empirical documents and that, like the literature discussed in the previous subsections, they therefore tend to reflect the impressionistic observations and preferences of those involved in their compilation. Whilst increased professional diversity in the panels of experts assembled to consult on such documents is therefore to be celebrated, there is still a clear need for empirical research.

The roots of the consensus statement on pregnancy loss terminology in English, though it was not labelled as a consensus statement and does not mention a consensus framework, appears to have been published in the journal *Human Reproduction* in 2005, on behalf of the European Society for Human Reproduction and Embryology (ESHRE) Special Interest Group on early pregnancy (Farquharson, Jauniaux, and Exalto, 2005). Here, Farquharson *et al.* provide what they term an 'updated glossary' to describe 'clinical events in early pregnancy' (2005, p.3008). They do this in the hope of 'facilitat[ing] the introduction of a revised terminology in an attempt to provide clarity and to enhance uptake and use in literature as well as clinical assessment and documentation' (2005, p.3008). This glossary suggests substitutions such as 'fetus' instead of 'embryo'; 'miscarriage' or 'termination of pregnancy', depending on context, instead of 'abortion'; 'empty sac' instead of 'anembryonic pregnancy' (p.3010), and 'gestational trophoblastic disease, complete or partial' instead of diagnoses containing 'mole' (p.3009).

With similar goals in mind and less than a decade later, a group of French clinicians published another document, again not labelled as a 'consensus statement' but this time compiled using a 'formal consensus method', which was intended to 'provide a standardised French/English terminology/glossary relating to pregnancy losses' (Delabaere *et al.*, 2014). Its main English-language recommendations are for *miscarriage* to be used with various modifiers to reflect the taxonomy of pregnancy loss they outline. The resulting labels include 'missed early miscarriage', 'incomplete early miscarriage', 'repeat miscarriage', and 'late miscarriage'. The following year, the ESHRE Special

Interest Group on early pregnancy updated its recommendations on diagnostic language, providing an explicitly labelled 'consensus statement'. This was produced with the aim of 'provid[ing] clear and consistent terminology for pregnancy loss prior to viability', and facilitating the comparison of study results between research centres (Kolte *et al.*, 2015). In a change that apparently reflects a wider trend towards *pregnancy loss*, Kolte *et al.* recommend both 'pregnancy loss' and 'miscarriage' (2015, p.496), and also endorse some labels discouraged by the previous ESHRE guidance (Farquharson, Jauniaux, and Exalto, 2005), such as 'anembryonic miscarriage' (Kolte *et al.*, 2015, p.496).

A more interdisciplinary consensus statement was published in 2020, to provide recommendations for delivery of unexpected news in Early Pregnancy Units and the Fetal Anomaly Screening Programme in NHS settings (Johnson *et al.*, 2020). These guidelines were reached via a workshop of 28 interdisciplinary healthcare professionals, policy experts, charity representatives, lay experts and academics, and consultation with a wider writing group of 39 individuals. Recommendations in relation to pregnancy loss include substitution of 'blighted ovum/anembryonic pregnancy' with 'a baby who died very early on', 'products of conception' with 'tissue/pregnancy tissue/remains of the pregnancy', and 'abortion' with 'miscarriage' (Johnson *et al.*, 2020).

Whilst not labelled as a consensus statement, the language guidelines circulated by the Royal College of Obstetricians and Gynaecologists in 2022, entitled 'RCOG Language Guide', seem to have been compiled using a similar model of consultation, though the disciplinary profile of those involved in their compilation is unclear. The RCOG's guidelines are intended 'to create consistency, fairness and inclusivity' (Royal College of Obstetricians and Gynaecologists, 2022). In relation to loss, they recommend substitution of 'incompetent cervix' with 'cervical dysfunction', 'spontaneous abortion/early fetal demise' with 'miscarriage', 'evacuation of retained products of conception' with 'surgical management of miscarriage' and 'parents who've suffered baby loss' with 'parents of a baby who died' (Royal College of Obstetricians and Gynaecologists, 2022).

Though all produced in the past 20 years, and all in the UK, with the exception of Delabaere *et al.* (2014) the publications highlighted in this subsection exhibit considerable inconsistency. Again, this underscores the need for empirical research to establish a basis for any linguistic reforms implemented, as well as to maximise the uptake, and impact on well-being, of any such initiatives. This need for empirical research is further reinforced by the apparently dated concept of how language is used in this domain. For example, *abortion* is repeatedly mentioned, despite little evidence of its continued usage in the UK in the context of pregnancy loss. Few participants in the research reported here recalled exposure to the word *abortion*, and recent quantitative research has found that only 14.2% of survey respondents who had experienced pregnancy loss in the first trimester of pregnancy in the UK since 2021 had heard or seen the word *abortion* in a clinical setting (Malory and Nuttall, 2024). Likewise, most of the consensus statements on this topic recommend *miscarriage* be used, despite the proliferation of challenges to its use documented in the previous section. Ultimately, therefore, such consensus documents capture only a partial, and often very partial, view of how language is used and perceived by those affected by pregnancy loss language. They benefit from the specialist expertise of clinicians, and in the case of Johnson *et al.* (2020), of a wider interdisciplinary team, but they fail to provide insights into usage and attitudes more broadly. The next section will outline how the research reported here, as well as other recent empirical linguistic research, has sought to combine the benefits of interdisciplinary collaboration and evidence-based recommendations.

2.4 Towards an Evidence Base

Previous subsections have highlighted the manifold challenges posed by pregnancy loss terminology, both in clinical and other specialist contexts and in wider society. This review of the literature has shown a clear need for rigorous, interdisciplinary empirical research to explore these challenges and provide evidence-based recommendations to facilitate any reforms indicated. Such a body of empirical research is now emerging, and the present study will make a significant contribution in this regard.

Recent studies provide compelling evidence of the damage which ineffective, insensitive, and unclear pregnancy loss terminology and discourses can cause. Such studies represent significant strides towards the extrapolation of empirical evidence to provide coherent, empirically derived recommendations for communicating about pregnancy loss. Brann, Bute, and Scott (2020), for example, provide some general recommendations which mirror advice on so-called 'reflective listening' which have gained traction in health communication advice in recent decades (e.g., Braillon and Taiebi, 2020). These include '[r]espond to patient cues' and '[p]rovide patients with full attention' (Brann, Bute, and Scott, 2020, p.262). Few recommendations made by Brann, Bute, and Scott (2020) are more specific, aside from one that will, by now, be familiar: '[a]void the term "abortion"' (p.264). Indeed, much of the empirical research on this topic seems to focus on *abortion*; both because there has been a dearth of empirical research on pregnancy loss terminology in British English and because the empirical research on American English reflects the more frequent use of *abortion* in loss contexts to this day.

With few empirical studies exploring language usage and preference in relation to pregnancy loss in recent years, and none presenting findings which are straightforwardly applicable to a UK context, we must look back to 2005 to consult the last empirical study of terminology use in pregnancy loss contexts in the UK. This was when Cameron and Penney (2005) conducted a case note review and survey in Scotland, to assess usage of four so-called 'inappropriate terms': *abortion, blighted ovum, incompetent cervix*, and *pregnancy failure* (p.314). Their findings reflect 'low levels of inappropriate terminology usage by health professionals' (Cameron and Penney, 2005, p.314), but they note that *pregnancy failure* was 'an exception', 'heard by approximately 1 in 7 women' (p.314) surveyed. The authors also report that '[r]elatively high levels of usage of 'abortion' were found in case records, with 1 in 10 hospital records containing this term' (p.314). Ultimately, they conclude that '[i]n order to meet national recommendations on terminology for early pregnancy loss, clinicians should not only say "miscarriage" but also write it' (p.314).

Similarly, *miscarriage* has repeatedly been shown to be a preferable alternative to *spontaneous abortion* in the handful of empirical studies on this topic conducted in a US context in recent years (Clement *et al.*, 2017; Clement *et al.*, 2019; Brann, Bute, and Scott, 2020). This is a frustratingly self-evident finding from a UK perspective, where *abortion* has, as outlined in previous subsections, been successfully eliminated in clinical contexts relating to pregnancy loss since the 1980s (Beard, Mowbray, and Pinker, 1985; Moscrop, 2013; Malory, 2022).

In the UK, few people experiencing pregnancy loss are now exposed to the word *abortion* in the context of their loss (Malory and Nuttall, 2024). Such differences in British and American English usage in this domain limit the applicability of US research findings to a UK context. A related issue with these studies is that when research participants are exposed to a highly stigmatised word like *abortion* (Malory, 2023), it risks a prejudicial ameliorative impact, whereby other variants seem less problematic by contrast. The ongoing scarcity of research informed by linguistic expertise and methodologies, which could take such effects into account, therefore limits the usefulness of much of this body of evidence. However, whilst insights as to the preferences of research participants in studies such as these must therefore be approached with caution, they provide the only recent data on attitudes to pregnancy loss terminology, and must be considered. The finding of Clement *et al.* (2019, p.4) that US '[p]articipants most frequently chose "miscarriage" as their preferred diagnosis term (n = 79 [54.5%]), followed by "early pregnancy loss" (n = 49 [33.8%])' is especially interesting, given the apparent preference of many writers discussed in previous subsections, in both the UK and the United States, for *pregnancy loss*. Clement *et al.* (2019) conclude that their 'data support that patients, too, prefer the term miscarriage to all other commonly used terms' (p.6), but do not make specific linguistic prescriptions.

However, whilst not focused on terminology, UK-based empirical research has seen significant strides being made in recent years in awareness of the importance of language for improving experiences of maternity care. The 'Death before Birth' project, whose findings were highlighted in Section 1.3, explored how those with lived-body experiences used figurative language to discuss their loss, highlighting how guidance such as patient information leaflets can most effectively present information on pregnancy loss (Austin *et al.*, 2021). Likewise, the Royal College of Midwives' 'Re:Birth' Project final report identified 'core principles' for healthcare professionals language usage during births (Royal College of Midwives, 2022, p.30). 'Re:Birth' did focus on clinical terminology, but reached the conclusion that 'we could not support or recommend the use of any particular term over another in conversation with women, birthing people and their families' (p.17), but that '[i]nstead, service user participants asked for health professionals to reflect the language they themselves used when speaking to them about their labours and births' (p.17).

Both 'Re:Birth' and 'Death before Birth' have made invaluable strides in demonstrating the importance of clinical communication to experiences of maternity care in the UK. Both also provide helpful models for empirically focused language research in a maternity context, as will be noted in Section 3. However, given that the 'Death before Birth' project was not focused on terminology and that 'Re:Birth' ultimately did not make terminological recommendations, as well as building upon these projects, this study also represents a departure from their research design. As noted in Section 1, a key principle underlying the research reported here is the need to focus both on lexical reform and the relationship between the lexical meaning of challenging diagnostic terminology and wider discourses which are experienced as challenging by people with lived experience of pregnancy loss.

Incidental linguistic findings such as those by Smith *et al.* (2020) in a sociological study about experiences of loss at the margins of the UK miscarriage/stillbirth threshold are likewise not oriented towards linguistic prescription. Smith *et al.* (2020) report that the word *miscarriage* poses a number of challenges when loss occurs later in the second trimester, but do not attempt to explore these challenges in depth, or to address how they might be ameliorated.

Previous subsections have shown that prescriptive recommendations for maternity terminology, such as those in the Peanut *Renaming Revolution: The Motherhood and Fertility Glossary* (2023), have been embraced wholeheartedly by some. However, researchers involved in gathering and presenting empirical evidence as to the impacts of terminology in maternity care, despite arguably being much better placed to make prescriptive recommendations, have tended to eschew this model of prescriptive recommendation.

The probable reasons for this reluctance are threefold. Firstly, and crucially, empirical research reflects a wide degree of variation in not only usage but also language attitudes and rarely results in clear consensus about particular words or phrases. Relatedly, with the exception of the 'Death before Birth' project, there has been an absence of specialist linguistic expertise in empirical research on this topic. Such expertise brings manifold benefits, including recognition that variation is expected, and can be expected to reflect 'ordered heterogeneity' (Labov, 1994, p.19), and advanced understanding of linguistic methodologies designed to capture both such heterogeneity in usage and in language attitudes. Such expertise is key to designing rigorous empirical research which can take account of variation and produce proportionate, evidence-based recommendations for linguistic reform where indicated. However, it seems likely that reluctance to prescribe specific linguistic variants amongst empirical researchers results, at least in part, from ongoing cultural squeamishness about breaching perceived professional boundaries of objectivity, including via linguistic prescriptivism. In the next section, this aversion to prescriptivism will be explored briefly, in the context of both historical developments in social science research generally and linguistics in particular, and the imperatives of linguistic reform of diagnostic terminology.

2.5 Time to Prescribe?

In the previous section, the absence of linguists from empirical research on the effects of terminology in maternity care was highlighted. Despite this, attitudes to prescriptivism from within the discipline of linguistics appear to have played a role in determining recommendations arising from such empirical research. These attitudes are shaped by the now-mainstream view in linguistics that language attitudes can have harmful impacts on a par with those of other forms of discrimination, and that prescriptive imposition of norms reflecting such attitudes can perpetuate prejudice and inequalities. This perspective risks impeding prescriptive interventions that could be socially progressive. As Malory (2025) highlights, prescriptivism is considered 'a crucial prejudicial mechanism' (p.624), thought to be 'tied up with intersectional language *prejudice*, understood as a bias, stigma, discrimination, or unfavourable treatment on the groups of language which renders some ways of speaking as illegitimate, as part of a racialised and classed pursuit of linguistic and biological purity' (Cushing and Snell, 2023, p.196; emphasis original).

Much less mainstream is the notion that prescriptivism, via 'language and the expertise of linguists can be used to *challenge* such hegemonic forces and subvert oppressive hierarchies' (Malory, 2025, p.623; emphasis original). In spite of this, as Wolfram and Schilling (2015, p.15) point out, whilst 'linguists studying language variation might be opposed to strands of prescriptivism that seem to reinforce and reproduce social inequalities in language', 'they have, at the same time, often taken an active role in politically responsive prescriptivism under the rubric of socially responsible "language reform"'. This is increasingly true, as Malory (2025) delineates. However, the view that prescriptivism is 'a four letter word' in academic contexts, and that 'it is neither desirable nor feasible to attempt to intervene in the 'natural' social life of language' (Edwards, 2012, p.17) continues to hold sway across linguistics and related disciplines. Together with corresponding concerns about maintaining 'objectivity' in social science research (Bird, 2020), this may explain the reluctance for authors of empirical research on pregnancy loss language to make concrete recommendations. Nonetheless, the ethical and methodological parameters of the 'politically responsive prescriptivism' Wolfram and Schilling (2015, p.15) discuss are being established within linguistics (Malory, 2023), and these allow for prescriptions grounded in empirical evidence gathered using robust linguistic methodologies.

Such linguistic methodologies, as well as linguistic expertise, are crucial in accounting for the complexities and nuances of individual contexts in which politically responsive prescriptivism might be beneficial. In the specific context of pregnancy loss terminology, it is vital that we uphold a distinction between contexts involving mass communication, where consensus on the least damaging terminology is necessary, such as policy documents and public health information, and contexts in which language use can be more responsive to individual preference. The need for a strategy which distinguishes between such contexts has informed the study reported in this Element, which aimed to develop a trauma-informed framework for supporting individual language preference in clinical interactions during and following pregnancy loss. This is distinct from related research designed to gauge usage and preference using a quantitative empirical model (Malory and Nuttall, 2024). That research is aimed at extrapolating quantitative findings to reach a clear, cohesive, standardised set of terminology for pregnancy loss which can function optimally across necessary mass communication domains, maximising clarity, and minimising distress (Malory and Nuttall, 2024).

Such approaches represent a departure from the fragmentary, discretely discipline-specific, focus of much of the literature highlighted in previous subsections. It is hoped that by introducing empirical linguistic expertise and facilitating a more joined-up, cohesive approach, involving a variety of stakeholders, the findings of this study can sustain multi-disciplinary attention to the problems of pregnancy loss terminology, and ask how language can best serve individuals affected by pregnancy loss, as well as clinicians, researchers, and wider society. As outlined in the previous section, resisting the fossilised misogyny of much of the terminology used around pregnancy loss, as well as the discourses that surround these words and phrases, is a pressing need.

Having established the need for a fresh methodological approach to the investigation of pregnancy loss language, the next section will introduce the dataset and method of analysis used in this study.

3 Data and Method

This study is based primarily on the examination of lived-body accounts of pregnancy loss and the role of language in these experiences. These accounts were gathered via focus groups and written contributions. This section will introduce the dataset, recruitment processes, ethical considerations, and collection procedures, as well as the analytical methods employed.

3.1 Data Collection

To collect primary data about experiences of language when receiving and delivering pregnancy loss care in a contemporary UK context, a series of 10 focus groups were conducted with 42 UK residents in May 2024. This model of data collection reflects the success of the participatory design used in the 'Death before Birth' project (cf. Littlemore and Turner, 2019, 2020), which used semi-structured interviews, but also the hope for a more discursive dataset in which participants would interact. Participants were recruited via social media and an online survey hosted in UCL's REDCap survey system, with recruitment assistance from the charities Tommy's, Sands, The Ectopic Pregnancy Trust, and Petals.

Prospective participants with lived experience of clinical pregnancy loss care in the 3 years since April 2021 were invited to anonymously complete a self-screening questionnaire, to assess their eligibility. Prospective participants whose professional role involved regular contact with people experiencing pregnancy loss were likewise invited to complete a separate self-screening questionnaire, to assess their eligibility. Table 1 details the study's inclusion criteria for both cohorts.

Having self-screened to determine their eligibility for participation, prospective participants were invited to submit a contact email address. Those who did were subsequently contacted and asked to complete a more detailed questionnaire which was designed to facilitate the grouping of participants with similar

Table 1 Study inclusion criteria for lived experience and healthcare professional cohorts

Lived experience cohort	Healthcare professional cohort
Bodily experience of pregnancy loss(es) between 2021 and 2024	Current employment in the UK health sector Professional role requiring regular interaction (>2 times per week) with people experiencing pregnancy loss OR who have experienced pregnancy loss within the last 3 years.

experiences for focus groups. Lived experience participants who determined themselves to meet the eligibility criteria were also invited to answer the question, 'Why would you like to take part in this study?'

A total of 290 prospective lived experience participants completed eligibility screening, with 237 submitting statements on their rationale for wanting to participate. These statements are the first source of lived experience data. Lived experience participants were then invited to complete the in-depth 'grouping' screening, also hosted in REDCap, to be assigned a Listening and Discussion Group or to contribute further in writing. The grouping questionnaire collected demographic information and gynaecological/obstetric history, as well as long-form responses to the prompt: 'Are there any issues or events related to language and pregnancy loss that you would particularly like to share during this project?' The data collected using this questionnaire facilitated the grouping of lived experience participants for focus group sessions, whilst also allowing those wishing to participate without taking part in a focus group to contribute substantively. A total of 110 lived experience participants completed the grouping questionnaire, with 98 writing statements about issues and events they particularly wished to contribute. These statements are the study's second source of research data.

Prospective healthcare professional participants who had self-screened for eligibility according to the inclusion criteria in Table 1 were also invited to complete a separate, in-depth, 'grouping' questionnaire for the purpose of assigning them to a focus group. This questionnaire collected professional background information, to facilitate the grouping of professionals with similar roles and responsibilities. Forty-nine healthcare professionals completed the eligibility questionnaire, and, of these, 42 submitted a contact email address and were sent invitations to complete the healthcare professional grouping questionnaire. Unfortunately, recruitment for the healthcare professional cohort proved challenging, and only 13 of 42 individuals invited to do so completed the grouping questionnaire. Like the lived experience grouping questionnaire, this allowed a long-form response to the prompt: 'Are there any issues, topics, or events related to language and pregnancy loss that you would particularly like to share during this project?' Ten healthcare professionals submitted statements in response to this prompt, and these are the third source of primary research data. All participants completing the grouping questionnaire gave consent for this data to be used and to participation in focus groups.

Ten focus group sessions were held in May 2024. Eight of these involved people with lived experience of pregnancy loss (n = 32), and two sessions involved people with professional experience of providing care during and/or after pregnancy loss (n = 10). The original study design involved 6 lived experience focus groups, with 30 lived experience participants; and 4 healthcare professional focus groups, involving 20 healthcare professional participants. However, the challenges of recruiting to the healthcare professional cohort, combined with over-subscription in the lived experience cohort, led to an adjustment in these targets. Using the grouping questionnaire data, participants were assigned to groups based on broad similarity of experience. This resulted in the focus groups outlined in Table 2.

Table 2 A breakdown of lived experience participant numbers in focus groups on first trimester loss, second trimester loss, Termination for Medical Reasons, and stillbirth, and healthcare professional participant numbers in focus groups on care during experiences of pregnancy loss and care following pregnancy loss

Lived experience cohort	Healthcare professional cohort
3 focus groups on first trimester loss (n = 14)	1 focus group for healthcare professionals involved in providing care during experiences of pregnancy loss (n = 5)
1 focus group on second trimester loss (n = 3)	1 focus group for healthcare professionals involved in providing after care following experiences of pregnancy loss (n = 5)
2 focus groups on Termination for Medical Reasons (n = 6)	
2 focus groups on stillbirth (n = 8)	
Total number of focus group participants: 32	Total number of focus group participants: 10

Five individuals were invited to attend each of the 10 focus groups, and given the choice of an in-person or online group. In line with mounting evidence that virtual focus groups allow participants to feel more comfortable when discussing sensitive topics (Papen et al., 2022), all focus group participants opted to attend online. Where an invitation was declined, another participant with similar experience was invited to fill a slot until each focus group had 5 confirmed attendees. However, the emotional burden placed on lived experience participants by the need to discuss trauma and bereavement in the focus groups led to an understandably high rate of non-attendance and last-minute withdrawals. Of the 40 lived experience participants confirmed to attend a focus group, 8 did not ultimately attend. This challenge was not mirrored in the healthcare professional cohort, where all confirmed attendees attended their scheduled focus group.

Focus groups were facilitated by the author, using prepared topic guides approved by the UCL Research Ethics Committee, when approval for data gathering was granted in April 2024 (26991/001). Support for project participants was provided by project partners Tommy's and Sands. Their helpline numbers were provided and helpline staff were notified in advance of focus group dates and prepared to support participants. All participants were offered a private debrief with the author, in addition to the group debrief that ended each focus group discussion.

During focus groups, lived experience focus group participants were asked about terminology used by clinicians to refer to their experience(s) of pregnancy loss and their babies, and how this made them feel, as well as their own preferred ways of communicating about these topics. Healthcare professional participants were asked in focus groups about language they use with people experiencing, or who have experienced pregnancy loss, as well as with other clinicians, and the factors determining such usage. Focus groups were recorded, using an encrypted audio recording device, and recordings were uploaded to UCL's Data Safe Haven and deleted from the recording device. In the Data Safe Haven, they were accessed by Research Assistant Eloise Parr, who produced verbatim transcripts for analysis by the author.

3.2 Participant Information

Demographic data about lived experience participants was gathered via the grouping questionnaire. These participants identified themselves as mostly being aged between 25 and 34 (n = 53), followed by 35 to 44 (n = 51) and 18 to 24 (n = 5). A significant majority of participants completing the grouping questionnaire selected 'woman' (n = 108) when asked to identify their gender. 1

participant selected 'non-binary' and 1 declined to provide their gender. Of the 32 lived experience participants involved in focus groups, 31 had selected 'woman' and 1 'non-binary'. 98.12% of participants (n = 101) completing the grouping questionnaire described themselves as heterosexual, 4.55% as bisexual (n = 5), and 1.82% as lesbian (n = 2).

Given disproportionate rates of adverse pregnancy outcomes amongst Black and Asian ethnic groups (Knight *et al.*, 2023), recruitment efforts focused on attempting to ensure representation for these communities. Charity and grassroots organisations focused on maternity inequalities were asked for recruitment assistance, and participants from racially minoritised communities underserved by the maternity system were prioritised for focus group places. Success with initial recruitment of minoritised populations was limited, with 82.73% (n = 91) of participants who completed grouping screening identifying their ethnic group as 'White'.[2] Only 3.64% (n = 4) of participants identified as 'Asian or Asian British', 1.89% (n = 2) identified as 'Black British, Caribbean or African', and 5.46% (n = 5) as 'Mixed or multiple ethnic groups'. This may reflect the significant reach of charity partners Tommy's and Sands, by comparison with the more limited reach of grassroots organisations focused on racially minoritised groups. Prioritising focus group places for lived experience participants of colour was a slightly more successful approach, as is shown in Figure 1. Of the 32 lived experience participants involved, 9.38% (n = 3) identified as 'Asian or Asian British', 6.25% (n = 2) as 'Black British, Caribbean or African', 9.38% (n = 3) as 'Mixed or multiple ethnic groups', and 3.13% identified themselves as 'Other ethnic group' (n = 2). The majority, 68.75% (n = 22), of participants thus identified as 'White', reflecting the limited success of attempts to recruit racially minoritised groups.

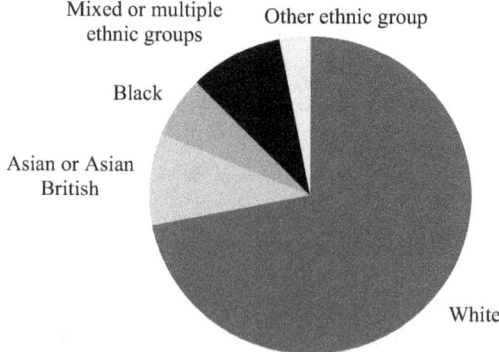

Figure 1 Ethnicity data of lived experience participants in focus groups.

---

[2] Ethnic group classifications were taken from the 2021 UK Census.

As will be outlined in Section 4, participants of colour reported specific challenges relating to pregnancy loss language in their communities. Future research must therefore do more to ensure representation from such communities. Demographic data was not collected from healthcare professional participants, who were required only to detail their professional background.

3.3 Data Analysis

Two methods of analysis were employed in this research; namely data-driven, inductive, qualitative thematic analysis focused on metalinguistic perception, and data-driven qualitative discourse analysis. The thematic analysis aimed to characterise attitudes towards, and effects of, pregnancy loss terminology amongst those affected by such language. It followed the six-step procedure framework for reflexive thematic analysis laid out by Braun and Clarke (2021): (1) familiarisation with dataset, (2) generating initial codes, (3) searching for themes, (4) reviewing themes, (5) defining themes, and (6) reporting findings. Familiarisation was undertaken via review of the transcripts and written contributions from the questionnaires. Initial colour codes were then assigned systematically, based on lexis and/or discourses identified as challenging by participants, and the effects participants associated with these. This process combined semantic and latent approaches to coding (Sekalala and Niezgoda, 2018, p.37). Coded data were then used as 'shorthand devices to label, separate, compile, and organize data' (Charmaz, 1983), to identify areas of similarity and overlap in order to generate themes and sub-themes. Whilst a data-led approach was taken during this phase of analysis, a scoping review and literature review had already been conducted and provided context for theme identification within the dataset. These themes were then reviewed against the coded dataset, to ensure that they meaningfully reflected the major topics of focus in the transcripts and written contributions, and that there was sufficient empirical basis for each of the themes identified. These themes were then refined, via selection of the data extracts to be analysed, and classified, in accordance with Braun and Clarke's step 5. At this stage, themes were defined and named, with linkages and patterns clarified in relationships between sub-themes and overarching themes. Finally, the results were summarised and a Final Thematic Map created to illustrate key aspects of the dataset in relation to the research questions and background literature.

The aim of this thematic analysis was to characterise attitudes towards, and effects of, pregnancy loss terminology and discourses amongst those directly affected by such language, both personally and professionally. By considering how language is appraised and functions in personal and professional contexts, this research sought to understand both why there have been persistent calls for linguistic reform in this context and the challenges involved. Following completion of the thematic analysis, the supplementary qualitative discourse analysis was conducted, with the aim of integrating micro-level analysis of metalinguistic effect with macro-level consideration of discursive constructs. The discourse analysis involved investigation of the data that considered how gendered identities are constructed and was underpinned by a feminist poststructuralist perspective (Weedon, 1997; Baxter, 2003) which views language as a social, context-bound phenomenon (Weedon, 1997).

Of interest here were the relationships between ideologies and identities and systems, structures, and processes governing healthcare experiences around pregnancy loss, and the analytical procedure used involved systematic analysis of lexis, syntactic structures, and discourse patterning which yielded additional insights beyond those facilitated by the earlier thematic analysis. As noted in Section 1, this Element builds on a tradition of previous work in Feminist Critical Discourse Analysis (FCDA) which aims to 'demystify the interrelationships of gender, power and ideology in discourse' (Lazar, 2005, p.5) and follows Sunderland (2000, 2004) in looking for lexico-grammatical patterns across texts, to determine how discourses can be 'traced'. In this study, the lexico-grammatical patterns that consistently yielded notable 'traces' of gendered discourses (Sunderland, 2004) were lexical repetition, patterns of transitivity, and representations of reported speech, and these are thus the focus of the findings reported in Section 5. Before this consideration of wider discursive representations around pregnancy loss, Section 4 will focus on the individual lexical units perceived to be associated with gendered difficulties by participants.

4 Pregnancy Loss Language and Notions of 'Good Motherhood'

The starting point for the empirical investigation of language used in pregnancy loss settings must be the experiences of people affected directly by pregnancy loss. This section will therefore present the findings of the study which relate to cultural expectations around 'good motherhood', before the next section considers themes emerging from the dataset which relate to the dismissal, sidelining, or undermining of pain reported by women and other misogyny-affected individuals.

There is a clear sense, across the dataset gathered during this study, that language can play a key role in experiences of healthcare associated with losing a baby during pregnancy. This is consistent with the limited insights afforded by previous empirical evidence (cf. Smith *et al.*, 2020), as well as the many anecdotal reports highlighted in Section 2 (e.g., Beard, Mowbray, and Pinker, 1985; Oré, 2020; Agg, 2023). Nonetheless, this is a significant and novel empirical finding. Outside clinical settings and in society more broadly, there is likewise evidence that some words and phrases play a role in perpetuating cultural taboos, misguided notions, and problematic narratives around pregnancy loss (Littlemore and Turner, 2019, 2020; Smith *et al.*, 2020).

The data gathered for this study contain many testimonies in which language is identified as a factor which impacted upon the emotional experience of pregnancy loss (unless explicitly labelled as a healthcare professional's contribution, 'HCP', all data extracts are from those with lived experience):

(4.01) 'I found the words used by others in the aftermath of my pregnancy so important and [they] really had an effect on how I dealt with the situation and my feelings.' (Written contribution)

(4.02) '[T]he language used by people involved in and around baby loss can have a huge impact on the mental health of those who are grieving.' (Written contribution)

(4.03) '[T]he way I was spoken to and [m]y baby was spoken about has had a profound and long lasting impact on how I have handled the loss ... I've found that the way people talk about my baby has a huge impact on my emotional response.' (Written contribution)

In addition to such general statements which posit a causal relationship between language and psychological well-being, many lived experience participants recalled specific incidents in which they felt language had been damaging:

(4.04) 'I found that the worst language was used by the surgeon that became involved in my care. I am a healthcare professional myself and was shocked at times. It contributed significantly to my emotional and mental distress.' (Written contribution; emphasis added)

(4.05) '[T]he language used when we spoke with our consultant after a missed miscarriage was discovered at our 12 week scan had a profound impact on our experience.' (Written contribution; emphasis added)

Whilst the majority of testimonies implicating language as influential in pregnancy loss experiences were negative, this was not universal. Several lived experience participants emphasised the power language has to mitigate the emotional impact of pregnancy loss, as well as to exacerbate it:

(4.06) 'Words have a lot of impact, we have had both positive and negative experience of this over the last few months since our baby died.' (Written contribution)

(4.07) 'Words hold power and during my experience the way I was spoken to and things were spoken about in a medical setting had a profound effect both negatively and positively.' (Written contribution)

(4.08) Language used can help or hinder loss parents significantly (Written contribution)

The sense in these participant testimonies, that language can play a key role in facilitating or impeding psychological recovery following pregnancy loss, was echoed by many participants in the health professional participant cohort. This impression was articulated with particular force by one healthcare professional participant who provides specialist counselling after pregnancy loss with the charity Petals:

(4.09) 'I'm thinking of Petals, we [have] limited [counselling] sessions and <u>you have to spend a lot of time trying to unpick the language</u> ... which actually interferes with the ... with supporting them with the loss, you know actually ... . there's time has to be spent on that piece of education, which actually that then is time away from other bits of therapy they could benefit from ... If we didn't have to spend that time ... you know, we could spend potentially four or six sessions, [and] we haven't got a lot of sessions, and if two or three of them are spent on unpicking the language, then that's even less with that couple or person. So then that impacts thinking about what's the impact [of the loss itself]. <u>[Language] has this ripple effect and it's a matter of undoing the language because maybe it's not considered or thought about</u> [in clinical settings].' (HCP focus group participant; emphasis added)

This identification of language as a significant factor in the experience of pregnancy loss was echoed by many other health professional participants:

(4.10) '[M]any mothers are upset by the way their pregnancy loss is referred to by medical staff and this can cause issues with grief for a long time. <u>I see clients years later who are still distressed by the language that was used.</u>' (Written contribution; emphasis added)

(4.11) 'I mean [I've seen] lots of really strong reactions, so where it's like ... I mean, even ... like terms like *retained products* is one. *Products* is a ... often a really sticky kind of word. <u>*Fetus* is very, for some people very triggering</u>. If they've had a termination and they've had to have an injection, then the paperwork will also potentially say *feticide* on there, or *infanticide*, and that's ... <u>that can really be hurtful. Hurtful is the word.</u> And, yeah, I think it's often just that they're the words that really, really stand out.' (Focus group participant; emphasis added)

These extracts from the dataset emphasise the long-term ramifications of poor language practice in the context of pregnancy loss. In many cases, participants used the word 'trauma' to describe these ramifications:

(4.12) 'Wording is so important. Words matter a lot. They can really help you deal with a traumatic event, or they can make it like even more traumatic if they're careless about it.' (Focus group participant)

(4.13) 'The language used during my first pregnancy loss was horrific and inappropriate. This led to increased trauma around my loss.' (Written contribution)

(4.14) 'Some [words] made our experience a lot easier ... whereas others really made a[n] already traumatic experience worse.' (Written contribution)

Such contributions make clear that language truly matters to many individuals who experience pregnancy loss and can play a crucial role in determining how they evaluate the care they receive during such experiences, and their subsequent well-being. In many cases, the impact of such language can be linked to normative gender role expectations internalised by participants, such as the notion of the 'good' mother introduced in Section 1.3. The thematic categories considered in the following subsections reflect this. Firstly, the next subsection will explore discourses of culpability and consideration by participants of terminology perceived to exacerbate a propensity for self-blame following pregnancy loss.

4.1 Culpability and Self-Blame

Over the past decade, a causative link between diagnostic language for pregnancy loss and the empirically established tendency for self-blame amongst people who have experienced this kind of loss has been hypothesised repeatedly in popular media. As outlined in Section 2, Canadian GP Iris Gorfinkel wrote in a (2015) newspaper article that people experiencing pregnancy loss 'largely continue to be under the false impression that the loss had been self-generated'; questioning whether the English-language word *miscarriage* could be 'partly to blame for these false impressions'. Broadening the scope of this argument beyond *miscarriage*, in an article in the UK's *Guardian* newspaper, journalist Katy Lindemann (2018) contended that:

> Our language of pregnancy loss is so wedded to the notion of failure, unintentionally attributing blame: 'failed pregnancy', 'incompetent cervix'. To a grieving mother, desperate for answers and quick to blame herself, even the term 'miscarriage' suggests her own inability to carry, as though she has somehow neglected her baby.

In *Life, Almost*, a book about pregnancy loss, journalist Jennie Agg likewise suggests a causative relationship between language and her personal experience of self-blame following recurrent first trimester losses:

> No wonder we have such a scrambled picture of cause and effect. Perhaps the first barrier to true understanding of miscarriage is a linguistic one. Because,

for all that some of the UK's best specialists can tell me, following the best available evidence, there is no inherent weakness or fallibility in my body that should hinder its ability to carry a baby. Yet, all the same, I can't shake the feeling that pregnancy is something I am just not very good at. (2023, p.144)

This widespread impression of a causative relationship between a lexical implication of responsibility or culpability and the psychological phenomenon of self-blame following pregnancy loss was shared by many participants in the study reported here. Echoing the findings of the 'Re:Birth' project (2022), which was introduced in Section 2, lexis implying failure was reported to be challenging in this regard. In the 'Re:Birth' report, the Royal College of Midwives team identified what they term the 'failure/incompetent words' as being amongst the 'difficult language' they considered (Royal College of Midwives, 2022, p.12). The 'Re:Birth' report thus concluded that when this kind of 'problematic language was used by others', it 'exacerbated an already challenging experience' for study participants (Royal College of Midwives, 2022, p.12). Like those of 'Re:Birth', the findings of the present study highlight that, almost two decades after Cameron and Penney found that the words *pregnancy failure* were 'heard by approximately 1 in 7 women' in their Scottish study (p.314), discourses of failure continue to be common in relation to pregnancy. This is an aspect of their lived experience that many participants reported as problematic:

(4.15) 'I really hated 'failing pregnancy'. I felt like it made me feel like a failure in a way I didn't until it was used.' (Written contribution; emphasis added)

(4.16) '[T]he language surrounding pregnancy loss needs reviewing, words like *miscarriage, incompetent cervix, placenta insufficiency* [sic], have such strong blame connotations and make a woman feel like she has failed in some way.' (Written contribution; emphasis added)

The notion that language can 'make [someone] feel like [they are] a failure', as expressed in data extract 4.15, can and has been applied to a significant proportion of the contemporary English pregnancy loss lexicon, including *pregnancy loss* itself. In 2011, Australian feminist sociologist Catherine Kevin published a paper which used the quotation 'I did not lose my baby . . . my baby just died' in its title, highlighting that questions of culpability apply too to the phrase *pregnancy loss*. This is despite relatively high approval ratings for *pregnancy loss* in recent UK-based quantitative research (Malory and Nuttall, 2024). Indeed, whilst most participants in the present study used *loss* to describe their experiences, project data also reflected the viewpoint that *loss* has connotations of negligence or carelessness. Several lived experience participants interpreted this as implying that they had *lost* their baby, in the sense of not knowing where it was, and associated the word with the implication of negligence:

(4.17) 'I don't like it when people say, '[Participant] lost the baby', 'cause I feel like they're saying <u>that I lost it, like I don't know where it was. I know where my baby was</u>. I didn't lose my baby.' (Focus group participant; emphasis added)

(4.18) '[A] lot of people use the language like, 'Sorry for your loss' ... I didn't really appreciate it 'cause again <u>I haven't lost anything. I definitely knew where my baby was</u>.' (Focus group participant; emphasis added)

These strikingly similar sentiments from different focus group sessions focusing on different types of experience (first trimester loss in the case of 4.17 and stillbirth in 4.18) suggest that these are not idiosyncratic responses, but rather reflect a wider experience in relation to the word *loss* in this context. Despite its conventionalised usage in other contexts of bereavement, participants explicitly linked the use of words related to *loss* to feelings of self-blame or negligence:

(4.19) 'I really hated when people said, 'I'm sorry for your loss'. I didn't lose something, my son died. <u>'I'm sorry for your loss' makes me feel like I am responsible</u>.' (Written contribution; emphasis added)

This rejection of *loss* may reflect the normative social expectations of 'intensive' (Hays, 1996) or 'total' (Wolf, 2007) motherhood, which cause loss to be experienced as failure. Interestingly, the participant quoted in extract 4.17 distinguished nominal *loss* from verbal *lost* in terms of implication of blame:

(4.20) ''Pregnancy loss' sounds like a noun ... but, <u>'You lost', it's like you've actively lost, it feels like the responsibility is on me</u>.' (Focus group participant; emphasis added)

This impression of language implying blame was also noted by participants in relation to *incompetent cervix* and *miscarriage*. Both these diagnostic labels have been highlighted repeatedly in the literature outlined in Section 2 as implying blame (Silver *et al.*, 2011; Gorfinkel, 2015; Oré, 2020), and this sentiment was echoed in the participant data:

(4.21) '[T]he word *miscarriage* to me <u>implies that you did something wrong</u>, that you mis-carried your baby.' (Focus group participant; emphasis added)

(4.22) '*Miscarriage* has a connotation that me carrying the baby ... <u>my carriage of it, I would say, is what is, what has gone wrong</u>.' (Focus group participant; emphasis added)

(4.23) 'I've always like hated, even before it happened to me, always hated the word *miscarriage* because <u>it sounds quite blamey</u> ... 'cause it's like 'oh the woman didn't carry the baby properly, your body mis-carried it', like you did something wrong.' (Focus group participant; emphasis added)

In 4.21–4.23, 'blaming' language is rejected because it is viewed as an external phenomenon implying responsibility. A distinction must be drawn between this perception of external blame and the internalisation of guilt and development of self-blame attributed to language. This causal relationship was posited in data extract 4.15, earlier, in which the participant says that *failing pregnancy* 'made me feel like a failure in a way I didn't until it was used' and 4.19, in which 'I'm sorry for your loss' is associated with an implication of responsibility. This relationship between diagnostic lexis and the development of self-blame is also explored in data extract 4.24:

(4.24)   'I don't like those terms [*weakened cervix* or *incompetent cervix*] 'cause it makes me feel as if . . . like the fault lies with me and . . . those types of words kind of added to my experience of feeling like shit, basically, that it's my fault . . . It's just not nice and . . . for baby loss I just don't think that word [*incompetent*] should be used at all.' (Focus group participant; emphasis added)

Here, the participant reflects on the impact that diagnostic language had on her experience and concludes that phrases like *incompetent cervix* exacerbated a propensity for self-blame. The participant testimonies considered therefore appear to reflect a spectrum of experience, ranging on the one hand from acknowledgement of the external phenomenon that some lexis implies guilt, to the perception that such lexis is directly responsible for feelings of responsibility which would otherwise not exist. Data extract 4.24 occupies an intermediate position on this spectrum, whereby a weaker, contributory, causal link is perceived to exist, with language exacerbating an existing tendency for self-blame, rather than suggesting blame where none would otherwise exist.

As highlighted in Section 2, such a causal link between lexis and self-blame is one that has been made repeatedly in the public domain over the last decade, especially in connection with the word *miscarriage*. Commentary on *miscarriage*, such as the viral 2018 Instagram post by former *Dawson's Creek* actor James Van Der Beek, demonstrate that the etymology of *miscarriage* and its literal meaning of 'failure to carry' are transparent to many non-linguists. For Van Der Beek, '"Mis-carriage", in an insidious way, suggests fault for the mother – as if she dropped something, or failed to "carry"' (quoted in Agg, 2023, p.142). This synonymity with failure was likewise highlighted by a participant:

(4.25) '[T]he word miscarriage in the thesaurus is synonymous with failure so when somebody says, '[Participant] miscarried', in my head, I hear, '[Participant] failed.' (Focus group participant)

Many participants in this study also felt strongly that *missed miscarriage*, a diagnostic term used to refer to a pregnancy which has stopped developing as expected but has not yet ended, implied culpability. This impression does not seem to be represented in previous discussions of pregnancy loss terminology but had clearly played a significant role in the experiences of several participants. Here, culpability is perceived to be implied by the adjective *missed* in the noun phrase *missed miscarriage*, with several participants parsing *missed* in this context not as adjectival but as a verb:

(4.26) 'It's obviously a massive shock because <u>yeah, you have missed it</u> ... missed miscarriage is like a horrible, horrible terminology.' (Focus group participant; emphasis added)

(4.27) '[I]t was a missed miscarriage and ... afterwards you know ... <u>there was some guilt, "so I missed it?"</u> ... it was a big thing, wave of guilt, you know like "I missed it".' (Focus group participant; emphasis added)

Again, a sense that this language directly contributed to feelings of self-blame and adverse psychological impacts also manifests in the dataset:

(4.28) 'I've been in counselling and stuff, um, and <u>I feel a lot of blame towards myself and I think, and I think, the language around missed miscarriage adds to that blame</u> ... It was kind of like, felt a lot like, "you've missed it, you must've seen something happening", when I went in for my scan and the- and they said ... they kept on saying, over and over and over again, "oh no, did you not have any symptoms? You must have had symptoms", and <u>then explaining it's a *missed miscarriage* and that I'd missed it. That language has really stuck with me</u>.' (Focus group participant; emphasis added)

As in extracts 4.26 and 4.27, the participant quoted in 4.28 clearly understands the meaning of the phrase *missed miscarriage* to be a pregnancy loss that *they* personally have missed. In this case, as in data extract 4.24, earlier, this phrase is perceived to play a contributory role, 'add[ing] to that [self-]blame'. Similarly, *empty sac*, a phrase used to describe anembryonic pregnancy, where a pregnancy is detectable via ultrasound but only the pregnancy sac and not its contents can be seen, was also considered to imply personal failure and to 'emphasise' self-perception of failure:

(4.29) '*[E]mpty sac* is really emphasises like, "Oh, I failed".' (Focus group participant)

Similar feelings were expressed in relation to the language used around experiences of Termination for Medical Reasons (TFMR). In a slight departure from the catalogue of diagnostic terminology for pregnancy loss linked with implications of culpability to this point, in this instance both the diagnostic terminology *termination* (as in 4.30) and discourses and modes of communication around TFMR (as in 4.31) were highlighted as factors contributing to self-blame.

(4.30) 'I think adding that word *termination* makes me feel guilty if that makes sense. Like ... I also just don't like say [*termination*]. I just wouldn't say it to someone if I was explaining what happened I wouldn't use that phrase [*Termination for Medical Reasons*].' (Focus group participant; emphasis added)

(4.31) 'I lost due to TFMR in 2023 ... the way I was spoken to, made me feel responsible for my daughters [*sic*] death.' (Written contribution; emphasis added)

For several participants, such feelings of culpability motivated avoidance of *termination*:

(4.32) 'I think that's probably why I prefer the phrase *compassionate induction*, because for me ... Everyone I speak to tells me not to be, but I am very, very guilty so I think that's why I sort of sway towards finding that easier to use than to say *termination*.' (Focus group participant; emphasis added)

As noted in Section 2, the phrase *compassionate induction* has been suggested repeatedly as an alternative (cf. Mobbs, Williams, and Weeks, 2018; Peanut, 2023) to TFMR, but concerns have been expressed that it does not clearly encapsulate all possible experiences of TFMR and that it could perpetuate stigma. The perceived stigma associated with some of the words and phrases used to diagnose and describe experiences of pregnancy loss was another theme which emerged strongly in the study reported here, and this theme will be explored in the next subsection.

Considerations of the role language plays in experiences of pregnancy loss, as an external accusation of guilt, exacerbating factor or causal influence in the development of feelings of self-blame, were echoed in the project data from healthcare professionals. This was a particularly salient theme in testimonies from those involved in providing psychological support following experiences of pregnancy loss:

(4.33) 'When we're at the receiving end, of taking in clients for baby loss work, they do feel ... the women, often particularly women, feel that they are to blame. That they've done something wrong. There's a guilt there. So, any of the language that presses into that is basically painful 'cause it ... sort of feels like that [is implied] then from a medical point of view. ... If the language isn't sensitive or considered, then it's just like a big fat arrow that says, "Yeah, you're to blame". Yeah, that's how people receive it and that just makes their, I think, their journey harder.' (HCP focus group participant; emphasis added)

In data extract 4.33, a healthcare professional participant considers the relationship between the self-blame of counselling clients who feel 'blame' and 'guilt' about their pregnancy loss, and the apparent external validation of language which 'presses into that' feeling, implying 'from a medical point of view' that they did 'do something wrong'. Ultimately, this participant concludes that such language functions as an exacerbating factor; a 'big fat arrow' that substantiates feelings of self-blame.

Though it may merely reflect the difficulties in recruitment of professional participants outlined in Section 3 and the correspondingly smaller number of participants (n = 13) in the healthcare professional cohort than the lived experience cohort (n = 290), it is perhaps significant that fewer diagnostic labels were associated with the implication of blame by healthcare professional participants. Whereas data extracts from lived experience participants have highlighted a perception that terminology such as *miscarriage, missed miscarriage, weakened/incompetent cervix, termination,* and others were associated with implied culpability, only *incompetent cervix* and *feticide* were explicitly raised in this context by healthcare professionals:

(4.34) '[I]t's not something that I would use [with a patient] ... I think it suggests a little bit of blame there doesn't *incompetence*? But it is the way that I would use [language when] discussing with clinicians.' (HCP focus group participant; emphasis added)

(4.35) '[*Incompetent* is] just a terrible word, isn't it? Because, you know, a woman, as a person is told that their body is *incompetent* ... It just feels like that is a personal thing. I think anything that has any element of blaming a body or a person just feels really ... um. Yeah, so *insufficient* feels more ... um, less ... blaming. [It] is just that the cervix doesn't hold that, and you know it's one of those things, rather than that you're not doing something right. So yeah, that's definitely a personal choice, but I think it is all my team. Nobody would use *incompetent* or *deficient* or anything.' (HCP focus group participant; emphasis added)

(4.36) 'Patients of mine who have requested notes and have been encouraged to open their notes have been absolutely blindsided and had no idea of that word [*feticide*]. Like, they've been told the baby needs an injection through the heart and that makes sense ... but it's so traumatic when that word is brought home because there's a lot of ... I would say guilt, feelings of guilt ... And when you use a word as strong as that, it's absolutely horrendous.' (HCP focus group participant; emphasis added)

In data extract 4.36, clinical terminology is once again implicated as a direct cause of guilt. In this case, issues with *feticide* experienced by this professional's patients seem to relate to the implication of agentive decision-making which will be discussed in the next subsection. Aside from this mention of *feticide*, only *incompetent cervix* is suggested by healthcare professional participants as terminology associated with blame. This may reflect a wider issue with clinical terminology, whereby healthcare staff can become desensitised to terminology which patients, being less (if at all) familiar with such language, find very challenging.

Data extract 4.34 also highlights the tension for healthcare professionals in pregnancy loss contexts of needing to separate a lexicon considered to be sensitive enough for patient-facing interactions from a lexicon optimised for comprehensibility, brevity, and transparency in clinician-to-clinician communication. Whilst this healthcare participant says they avoid using *incompetence* because it 'suggests a little bit of blame', they note that this is the way that they would use language when 'discussing with clinicians'. In relation to this need for two tiers of lexis, one for patient-facing interactions and one for clinical communication, several healthcare professional participants highlighted the competing imperatives involved:

(4.37) 'I think something that can be hard is that from maybe a midwife point of view is that you're using <u>certain language to make sure you get clarity between professionals and other language to make sure you meet someone's emotional needs</u> and so using the wrong legal definition or clinical definition can cause harm not in terms of you know if a referral was made where someone does have cervical insufficiency ... it needs to be clear what that referral is referring to, so they don't miss out on scans when they need them. Whereas if ... we called a baby who has died under 24 weeks a *stillbirth,* they are potentially going to be referred to a rainbow clinic where scans start at 23 weeks [whereas] in a preterm birth clinic where miscarriages are monitored in a subsequent pregnancy, there it's probably 9 weeks earlier that the scans need to start. So <u>language that determines clinical pathways needs to be really specific and is often not the language that we would want to use with families</u> and yet if we use language that families use in those settings we potentially risk missing people, missing care.' (HCP focus group participant; emphasis added)

(4.38) '[S]ome documents are legal documents, so if somebody is having a Termination for Medical Reasons [involving feticide], <u>the word *feticide* is a legal requirement to write.</u> [I]f you write [something vague like] *injection,* then your form will be rejected because it could be any injection, [it] could be a water injection ... .' (HCP focus group participant; emphasis added)

Data extracts 4.37 and 4.38 highlight the complexities of sensitive communication for clinical staff, whether in relation to 'blaming' language such as *incompetent* or *feticide*, or taxonomising language such as *miscarriage/stillbirth*, which will be discussed in Section 5. These extracts highlight the importance of specificity in clinical language, both to ensure clinical pathways are followed for optimal patient safety and to ensure compliance with legal requirements, and the difficulty of reconciling sensitivity to patient needs with clinical clarity.

The participant testimonies laid out in this subsection so far have shown clearly that diagnostic lexis, such as *miscarriage, loss, failure, incompetence*, and *termination*, is perceived by some people experiencing pregnancy loss, as well as some of those providing healthcare for them, as implying blame. Even more concerningly, the testimonies cited here have demonstrated that many lived experience participants posit a causal link between their self-blame for the loss and the clinical language used in connection with their experience. This belief of personal responsibility reflects a wider cultural tendency to presuppose 'that women's bodies alone are responsible for the fate of a pregnancy' (Agg, 2023, p.150). This propensity to 'locate the activities and consequences' of pregnancy risk 'at the level of the individual' is also explored by Johnson and Quinlan (2019, p.67) in relation to highly influential pregnancy advice manuals such as *What to Expect when you are Expecting* (Murkoff, 2018). For Johnson and Quinlan, this intense 'focus on individual responsibility for pregnancy outcomes increases the policing of pregnant bodies' (Johnson and Quinlan, 2019, p.67). This focus is also bound up with the normative discourses of 'good' motherhood, which is 'intensive' (Hays, 1996), 'total' (Wolf, 2007), 'child-centric' (Mackenzie, 2018), and self-sacrificing from pregnancy onwards, which were explored in Section 1.3. As was noted there, a perhaps inevitable concomitant of this presupposition of individual responsibility – and the policing it results in – is the priming of women and birthing people to internalise the 'blaming' language they are exposed to. This facilitates the transition discernible in data extracts in this subsection, from awareness that language can seem to exemplify an external accusation of responsibility, to the internalisation of that blame by some lived experience participants.

Discourses of culpability which locate responsibility for pregnancy loss with the pregnant body also reflect what Barad (1998) has labelled 'hyper-maternal responsibility', whereby 'real questions of accountability' are displaced onto the pregnant woman who is actively constructed as a 'mother' bearing 'full responsibility, and the full burden of accountability, for fetal well-being' (p.116). This is despite a growing body of evidence which shows that social determinants of health which are 'not modifiable by individual behaviour' (Eger, 2023) play a much more significant role in pregnancy outcomes than individual behaviour change (Bohren *et al.*, 2024; Yip *et al.*, 2024). This 'unreasonable' level of 'maternal accountability', as it is labelled by Talbot (2018, p.103) is usually considered in terms of its ramifications in abortion debates, but it has consequences in contexts of pregnancy loss too. In relation to pregnancy loss, it is easy to see how the problematic notion of 'good motherhood' as self-sacrificing and all-consuming (Miller, 2023, p.15) and 'compulsory motherhood' (Ellece, 2012) or the so-called 'motherhood mandate' (Russo, 1976), 'a form of pro-natalism that dictates the requirement that to be a "real" or "good" woman, one must be a good mother' (Klann and Golabi, 2024, p.178), can result in guilt and self-blame when pregnancy loss occurs. This impact is then exacerbated by language felt to blame, such as *failure, miscarriage, incompetent, missed*, and *termination*. Following Martin (2001), Kinloch and Jaworska (2021) argue that biomedical vocabulary of this sort imposes an understanding of pregnancy which 'views the female body as a "machine"' required to 'perform its reproductive "function" well' (3).

Looking beyond individual lexical units, moreover, discourses of pregnancy 'failure' can function to objectify the pregnant body and imply its sole raison d'etre is to procreate. In data extract 4.39, for example, a lived experience participant reports the use of a metaphor by a healthcare professional which functions in this way:

(4.39) 'When I found out my baby had no heartbeat the consultant said to me, "Think of it like a manufacturing production line and your body is getting rid of defective product".' (Written contribution; emphasis added)

In this data extract, the objectification of this participant's body is clear: she is 'a manufacturing production line' which is 'getting rid of defective product'. Whilst we cannot possibly know what prompted this healthcare professional to make this horrifying comparison, it is interesting and potentially significant that they use the word *product*, a common way of referring to retained tissues during or following experiences of pregnancy loss, either on its own or as an element of the multi-word unit *products of conception*. This begs the question, does use of such semantically broad terminological labels as *products*, which are equally applicable in the context of a manufacturing line as in the context of a pregnancy loss consultation, predispose clinicians to regard their patients as 'manufacturing production line(s)'? As noted in Section 1.1, this question, like those of the causal relationship perceived by some participants to exist between 'blaming' language and self-blame, steers us close to questions about whether language can determine what we perceive and to the Sapir-Whorf hypothesis. As outlined in Section 1.1, whilst a 'pure' form of the Sapir-Whorf hypothesis has now largely been rejected by linguists and cognitive scientists, a 'weaker form' of linguistic relativity (Graumann, 2007, p.134) is widely accepted. This watered-down version of the Sapir-Whorf hypothesis 'suggests that recurrent patterns of language use may predispose speakers to view the world in particular ways, but that such a worldview is not all-determining' (Ehrlich, 2003, p.13), and this does seem to be reflected in much of the dataset presented here. It may thus not be a huge leap to ask whether words like *product* may have such an objectifying effect on cognition for clinicians.

Questioning the relationship between specific words and overarching discourses also leads us to confront another thorny issue raised in Section 1.1; of whether, in the words of Deborah Cameron, 'replacing one [lexical] form with another may eliminate overt or surface bias' but not the discourses which accompany, and ultimately gave rise to, individual words (Cameron, 2023, p.16). Cameron raises this issue in the context of anti-sexist language initiatives, noting that

> In real life, words do not exist in isolation: rather we encounter them in the social contexts where they are used to say and do things – or, put another way, in *discourse*. Historically, sexist language is a product of sexist discourse: a word like *spinster*, for instance, which was once just a neutral term denoting a not-yet-married woman, must have developed its current, negative associations through being used repeatedly in discourse that represented unmarried women in negative ways. And discourse can be sexist without containing sexist language. (Cameron, 2023, p.16)

Whilst it is undoubtedly true that often, as Cameron puts it, 'the problem itself goes deeper' (Cameron, 2023, p.16), in many cases, than surface lexis, this is heavily context-dependent. In many instances of linguistic reform, as Cameron notes, 'attempts to change language don't usually succeed unless the beliefs they embody or affirm have already achieved a certain level of acceptance in the community', meaning that '[t]he discourse [has] to change before the linguistic reform could be successful' (Cameron, 2023, pp.171–172). However, in light of consistent evidence presented in this subsection that pregnancy loss terminology is perceived to make those experiencing loss 'feel like a failure in a way [they] didn't until [such language] was used' (data extract 4.15), we must question whether discourse has either already changed, or is in the process of changing, and whether as a result, the fossilisation of culpability into words such as *miscarriage* and *incompetent* is perpetuating or re-imposing a sense of failure that may otherwise not be felt.

Having explored, in this subsection, the thematic category of culpability that emerged in the dataset, and its relationship to the gendered notion of 'good' motherhood (Miller, 2023, p.15), we will now turn in the next subsection to the theme of stigma, which is likewise closely related to gender role expectations and maternal ideals.

4.2 Stigmatising Lexis

In recent years, there have been a number of attempts to raise consciousness of the stigma and societal taboo associated with pregnancy loss in the UK. In the public domain, national charities such as Tommy's and Sands have run campaigns aimed at destigmatisation, and empirical research such as Littlemore & Turner (2020) has highlighted the importance of cultural scripts for challenging societal taboos. Much has also been written on the so-called inter-cultural 'social awkwardness' which pregnancy loss often poses (Andipatin, Naidoo, and Roomaney, 2019), since different cultural norms pose different and, often intersecting, difficulties for those experiencing pregnancy loss (Tommy's, no date). In light of the disproportionate rate of adverse pregnancy outcomes amongst Black and Asian ethnic groups and those from deprived socioeconomic backgrounds (Knight *et al.*, 2023), there is clearly an urgent need for research exploring the experiences of pregnancy loss communication for these groups. As Lacci-Reilly *et al.* (2023) note in relation to Black, Indigenous and People of Colour (BIPOC) groups in the United States, particular attention needs to be paid to 'cultural considerations and discrimination in the healthcare setting' in such communication-focused research (p.6).

More consideration is also needed of the ways in which media, both traditional and social, contribute to stigmatising and/or destigmatising pregnancy loss, since recent research indicates that traditional media may perpetuate problematic conceptions of pregnancy loss. Martin (2023) finds that although there has been a notable increase in public discourse about experiences of pregnancy loss, news media coverage often perpetuates heteronormative and male chauvinistic narratives and sensationalises such experiences. The role social media plays, as a forum for opinion-sharing about pregnancy loss terminology, was discussed in Section 2.1, particularly in relation to the 'wave of conversation' (Oré, 2020) which often follows a major news story about a celebrity who has experienced pregnancy loss. The death of Chrissy Teigen and John Legend's son Jack at around 20 weeks of pregnancy represents a particularly significant instance of this phenomenon, since Jack's gestational age ignited debate about the applicability of the term *miscarriage* in the second trimester. Further public discussion ensued when Teigen clarified in 2022 that she now conceptualised her experience as 'an abortion to save my life for a baby who had absolutely no chance', in an attempt to challenge stigma around reproductive freedoms in the aftermath of the US Supreme Court's decision to overturn *Roe vs. Wade* (*BBC News*, 2022).

Language, Gender, and Pregnancy Loss

As Teigen's clarification highlights, the issue of stigma relating to pregnancy loss is particularly important when a loss is perceived to be associated with choice or decision making, such as TFMR. As will be clear from the following participant contributions, the homonymity of *termination* in British clinical English, which is used in both the phrase *Termination of Pregnancy*, which has replaced *abortion* to refer in clinical settings to the termination of unwanted pregnancies (Kavanagh and Aiken, 2018; Steer, 2018) and *Termination for Medical Reasons*, to refer to the loss of a wanted pregnancy due to medical complications or anomalies, is often perceived to create or sustain the association of *TFMR* and stigma.

(4.40)   'I've shied away from using *termination for medical reasons* I have to say. I think it can be ... I think the word *termination*, unfortunately, <u>it can invoke a number of different emotions can't it, for different people and there are people who I know have very strong beliefs around termination generally and the fact that, you know, you shouldn't be allowed at all</u>, you know, so I've shied away from that.' (Focus group participant; emphasis added)

(4.41)   'The word *termination* just, for some reason, doesn't sit right for me ... for some reason. But again, I think that's our experience ... but <u>I also grew up in a Catholic household and went through Catholic schools, who have sort of drilled in from a very young age that you know</u> ... so I think it depends on your personal experience with that language and so on.' (Focus group participant; emphasis added)

For both participants quoted here, the word *termination* cannot be divorced from its association with abortion of unwanted pregnancies. The participant quoted in extract 4.40 highlights awareness of some 'people who I know have very strong beliefs' that abortion 'shouldn't be allowed at all', whilst the participant quoted in extract 4.41 relates her dislike of the word *termination* to her Catholic upbringing and messages about abortion that were 'drilled in[to her] from a very young age'. In both cases, there is an implication that their experiences of TFMR are not sufficiently clearly differentiated in language from the termination of an unwanted pregnancy for *termination* to be a palatable diagnostic label. Along with linguistic efficiency, this may also be a motivating factor for use of the acronym *TFMR*, rather than the expanded phrase *Termination for Medical Reasons*. Whilst this difficulty with *termination* prompted most participants to avoid or minimise their use of the word, it notably had the opposite effect for one participant, who felt that the stigma associated with *termination* motivated her to use the word more frequently, in order to highlight the importance of TFMR as reproductive healthcare:

(4.42) 'I find myself, since everything that is happening in America with Roe vs. Wade being overturned, I've actually found myself using the word *termination* a lot ... I'm like, "Termination is ... I've literally had three for two wanted pregnancies!"' (Focus group participant; emphasis added)

In data extract 4.42, the quoted participant is clearly aware of the potential risk for stigma to be perpetuated if others have the impression that *termination* occurs only in the context of unwanted pregnancy. This, of course, raises questions as to whether broader efforts to destigmatise the exercise of reproductive freedoms are needed, and the role language might play in such efforts, but these are beyond the scope of this Element.

The word *abortion* was also strongly associated with negative responses amongst those with lived experience of pregnancy loss in which it had arisen:

(4.43) 'The woman who I was discussing my procedure with kept referring to it as an *abortion* ... but I wasn't having an abortion [crying] my baby [crying] was already gone.' (Focus group participant)

Likewise, the word *feticide* was identified by several participants as extremely challenging:

(4.44) '[I]n the end, they technically died with a procedure called a *foeticide* [sic], which is a hard word. This was referred to as an *abortion* on my paperwork.' (Written contribution)

(4.45) 'During my loss later on at almost 24 weeks, I hated the term *feticide* which is what we had to do before being induced. I hated any reference to the word *abortion*.' (Written contribution)

Study data indicate that the vehement rejection of *termination*, *abortion*, and *feticide* by participants is related to their association with intentional acts, as well as stigma associated with those acts. This was expressed explicitly where words such as *termination* and *abortion* were considered by several participants to posit the existence of choice where none was perceived to exist:

(4.46) 'It was a loss of a baby that I wanted and so, that was the struggle for me around the language that was there, of saying *termination* when actually it feels like the choice was not there.' (Focus group participant; emphasis added)

(4.47) 'When I was medically discharged, the pill they gave me was obviously the abortion tablet. And I remember the midwife didn't tell me that, but it was in a leaflet I read and that was bad ... I remember reading the words on the leaflet when they kind of explained what was going on ... and I remember thinking, "But I'm not choosing this. This is not ... I'm not taking this because it's a choice", and, and it did make me feel very guilty, even though my brain knew that I had to do it ... it's the guilt like, "I'm taking this". I haven't, they didn't use the word [abortion] which I'm really thankful for but I ... I did still read it.' (Focus group participant; emphasis added)

In data extract 4.47, as in the previous subsection, a participant posits a causal link between an individual lexical item and feelings about their loss experience. This was also reflected in discussions about the word *choice* itself, which several participants who had been through TFMR or medical/surgical management for loss considered to be strongly associated with free preference, rather than the constraints of their loss experience:

(4.48) 'People find it incredibly triggering, the word *choice*, definitely. Incredibly triggering, because I guess you're left thinking, "well this would never be my choice, this situation has never been my choice, so it's not really a choice", so yeah that is, it is a challenge.' (Focus group participant)

As in the previous subsection, this does seem to be an issue with the single, specific, word, *choice*, though of course this is in the context of wider discursive representations of TFMR. In one focus group discussion, lived experience participants with a history of TFMR had an extended discussion about whether *decision* might be less objectionable than *choice* in clinical settings when TFMR is being discussed:

(4.49) 'I'm stumbling a bit because I feel like in some ways in those heightened times of emotion it's going to be very difficult to use a single word or you know a single phrase that's gonna make anyone feel better ... I probably would replace the word *choice*, definitely. I think a *decision*, I think yeah, it's a *decision* that in some cases needs to be made for sure.' (Focus group participant; emphasis added)

(4.50) 'I did use the word *decision*, actually, around whether or not continuing with the pregnancy was the right thing to do for [baby], and for us as a family ... I really used, used those terms, *decision* definitely actually ... and I said [to people], "Ultimately ... we've decided that we don't think [continuing with the pregnancy is] the right thing to do".' (Focus group participant; emphasis added)

In data extract 4.49, the participant initially expresses doubt as to whether 'a single word' can 'make anyone feel better' in such a traumatic situation, before deciding that *decision* should in fact replace *choice*, and by implication that it can. In data extract 4.50, this preference for *decision* over *choice* is reflected; here, the participant realises that they did use the word *decision* in explaining to family and friends what had happened. Whilst other participants with experience of TFMR used the word *choice* without apparent difficulty, it did emerge as a lexical unit identified as 'triggering', as in 4.48, by a number of lived experience participants. This seems to relate to the discourses of constraint exemplified in the data extracts in this subsection, by statements such as 'the choice was not there' in 4.46.

Whilst the distress caused by any perceived implication of freedom of choice in contexts of medical/surgical management or TFMR is likely to be related in large part to the painful irony of feeling powerless but being ascribed agency, the data presented in this subsection indicate that societal stigma around the choice to terminate unwanted pregnancies also plays a role. As in the previous subsection, expectations of motherhood as 'intensive' (Hays, 1996), 'total' (Wolf, 2007), 'child-centric' (Mackenzie, 2018), and even 'compulsory' (Ellece, 2012) are pertinent here, since '[p]eople who have abortions may be seen as violating a feminine requirement to be caring, motherly and self-sacrificial, especially given the anti-abortion rhetoric that paints those who access abortion as cruel, uncaring, or murderous' (Klann and Golabi, 2024, p.178).

Given that studies of abortion stigma have demonstrated that reproductive rights are discussed in terms of violating gender norms and rejecting gender role expectations (Kumar, Hessini, and Mitchell, 2009; Baker *et al.*, 2023), it seems unsurprising that any implied or lexical overlap between termination of an unwanted pregnancy and one experienced as a loss either with no element of choice or a very constrained element of choice, would pose difficulties for lived experience participants. This is made clear by contributions such as 4.40 and 4.41, which indicate a conscious desire to avoid using lexis associated with the semantic overlap between termination of unwanted and wanted pregnancies due to awareness of stigma and strength of anti-abortion sentiments, as well as by references to experiences of TFMR in which participants and their families had had to make decisions around quality of life for their baby if the pregnancy continued:

(4.51) 'I've entered into to some mental health support afterwards – so I was diagnosed with PTSD – and [*compassionate induction* is] the terminology that the trauma-informed maternal services, that they've been using with me. And it just seems much kinder … it seems, for me it sounds softer, it feels softer. And that idea of it being, like, compassionate makes it seem like, you know, it wasn't us thinking that we couldn't cope with [baby] and so on. It was actually just … just the situation put onto us.' (Focus group participant; emphasis added)

(4.52) '[I]t makes my skin crawl when people are like, "Oh, well, better make sure you wear protection!" … This was all in the name of healthcare for myself and for my family and, compassionately, for my baby at Christmas. I couldn't have got pregnant again with the second baby if I hadn't had the surgical termination, because I was so ill after the medical termination the first time!" ... So, if you are "pro-life" or pro- whatever ... I find it really difficult when stuff like that is online ... and <u>as much as it's, you know, it is my body and it is my choice, I'm still like</u>, "That is a massive part of healthcare [for people] who are trying to have families!"' (Focus group participant; emphasis added)

In data extract 4.51, the participant discusses the difficulty of navigating language around their experience of TFMR. For them, *termination* carries the implication that they 'couldn't cope with [baby]' and the medical anomalies identified via ultrasound during the pregnancy, whereas *compassionate induction* is perceived to recognise that this was 'the situation put onto us' and foregrounds the limitations of their agency in the situation. This sentiment is echoed in data extract 4.52, in which the participant refers to their terminations as 'healthcare for myself and my family and, compassionately, for my baby at Christmas'. Data extract 4.51 also invokes pro-choice discourses, saying 'as much as it's ... my body and it is my choice' but differentiating her situation from the exercise of reproductive freedom and emphasising the constraint on her choice. These contributions thus both stress that TFMRs are 'compassionate', situating themselves in relation to notions of self-sacrificial motherhood and thereby rejecting the implication that their TFMR involved violation of the 'feminine requirement to be caring, motherly and self-sacrificial' (Klann and Golabi, 2024, p.178) and arguing instead that their 'compassionate" choice fulfils this 'requirement'. In data extract 4.52, by saying, '[I]t makes my skin crawl when people are like, "Oh, well, better make sure you wear protection!"', the participant also draws upon another aspect of abortion stigma; its association in the public consciousness in some domains with "promiscuity, irresponsibility, and sin"' (Hanschmidt *et al.*, 2016). Once again, this taps into the normative discourse of 'good' motherhood, reflecting what Mackenzie (2023, p.90) refers to as 'oppositional constructions of "ideal" or "good" versus 'problematic' or 'bad' motherhood' and arguably sustaining stigma around reproductive choice.

Lived experience participants' testimonies thus reflect a perception that there is insufficient differentiation between language used around termination of an unwanted pregnancy and language used in contexts of pregnancy loss, such as medical or surgical management for incomplete pregnancy loss and procedures for Termination for Medical Reasons. This perception is also reflected in healthcare participant contributions; several healthcare professional participants highlighted stigma associated with this semantic overlap as a factor that had contributed to negative experiences for patients:

(4.53)   'Lots of women have said to me, "But then I had to say straight away, you know, when I came round [from anaesthetic], the first thing I said to whoever the medical staff was at the time is that I didn't ... I really wanted this baby". You know, that ... they don't want to be judged, that they ... they wanted the baby. And if I'm thinking about the language around termination specifically it's a broad brush, isn't it? Everything's under that umbrella and there can be the ending of a pregnancy for a number of reasons, but it feels like there's a really apologetic explanation that has to come tumbling out, sometimes, of women who feel that the negativity of that word ... for them, [the word *abortion* is] almost saying ... "You've had an abortion. You didn't want to have this baby".' (HCP focus group participant; emphasis added)

In data extract 4.53, this healthcare professional highlights the fear of judgment and stigma associated with the word *abortion* for patients who undergo surgical management for incomplete pregnancy loss or TFMR. It is unclear whether this sense of stigma is associated with a perception of strong views on reproductive rights, or whether it merely reflects a desire to stress that a lost baby was 'really wanted'. Elsewhere in this subsection, though, themes of culpability and stigma arising from the metalinguistic commentaries of lived experience participants have been explored and situated in relation to societal expectations of 'good' motherhood. It is apparent from the testimonies of lived experience participants quoted throughout this section that the negative impacts of pregnancy loss terminology and discourses they have experienced can often be related to the perception that their loss is perceived as a failure to perform adequately in safeguarding their baby, or an active rejection of the maternal role. In relation to discourses of culpability and terminology perceived to imply blame, this sense is associated with both rejection of language felt to imply negligence and with internalisation of self-blame following loss. In relation to the stigma associated with the semantic overlap between abortion for unwanted pregnancies and procedures around pregnancy loss involving words like *termination* or *abortion*, participant testimonies demonstrate an awareness of anti-abortion sentiments and a desire to both distance their experiences from the termination of unwanted pregnancies and to highlight their fulfilment of a traditional nurturing maternal role which exists in opposition to cultural stereotypes of uncaring and promiscuous women who seek abortions for unwanted pregnancy.

In addition to the themes of culpability and stigma which emerged from the study dataset and relate to gender norms and notions of the 'good' mother, another set of themes also emerged. These relate to the dismissal, sidelining, or undermining of pain reported by women and other misogyny-affected individuals, and are the focus of the next section.

5 Pregnancy Loss Language and the 'Gender Pain Gap'

Participant data presented in the previous section made clear that language can play a key role in experiences of healthcare associated with losing a baby during pregnancy. This is consistent with the limited insights afforded by previous empirical research (e.g., Smith *et al.*, 2020; Turner *et al.*, 2020; Kraus, 2022) and the numerous anecdotal reports (e.g., Beard, Mowbray, and Pinker, 1985; Oré, 2020; Agg, 2023) highlighted in Section 2. In Section 4, the impact of such language was considered in relation to cultural expectations of motherhood, and the normative ideal of maternal responsibility implied by discourses around, and terminology associated with, culpability for pregnancy loss and stigma around assumptions of choice and agency in experiences of loss. Whilst, as was demonstrated in the previous section, a clear link can be discerned between negative experiences of communication around pregnancy loss and these normative ideals of motherhood, other themes also emerged in the participant testimonies collected for this study. These relate to the dismissal, underestimation, or undermining of pain by women and other misogyny-affected individuals and are explored in the following subsections.

5.1 Hierarchies of Grief

The concept of 'disenfranchised grief', where 'grief [is] experienced by those who incur a loss that is not, or cannot be, openly acknowledged, publicly mourned or socially supported' (Doka, 1999, p.37), has been discussed extensively in relation to pregnancy and baby loss. This is because, according to Robson and Walter (2013), there exist types of loss 'that are entirely unrecognised socially, such as miscarriage or elective abortion [*sic*]' (p.109). Introducing the concept of 'hierarchies of loss', Robson and Walter (2013) reject the 'binary assumption that grief is either enfranchised or disenfranchised', arguing that 'social norms about the legitimacy of bereavement are not binary (yes-no), but are scalar or hierarchical' (p.97). Robson and Walter (2013) therefore propose a tool for 'identifying hierarchies of loss' (113). In adapting this framework to the specific context of miscarriage and TFMR, in order for such 'experiences which fall outside assumed norms [to] be included and examined', Middlemiss and Kilshaw (2023, p.2) find that 'there are indeed hierarchies of loss based on some persons being afforded more social legitimacy in their reaction to loss'. According to Middlemiss and Kilshaw (2023) the hierarchisation of pregnancy loss is influenced by factors such as 'gestational time' (p.15), with longer pregnancies preceding loss being afforded greater social legitimacy. They also note that individuals can 'recognise and use hierarchies of loss in agential ways, sometimes to convey the impact and bolster the social status of their own loss, sometimes to assert the legitimacy of the foetal being or baby that died' (p.15). These findings were reflected in the dataset for the study reported here, for example in the testimonies of participants who had experienced full- or near-term stillbirths, and who felt strongly that the gestational age of their baby was a fundamental aspect of the experience that they wanted to emphasise in the language they used:

(5.01) 'I'm not totally happy with the word *stillbirth* and I think my reason is because it encompasses such a range of loss, and <u>I always really feel like I need to tell people that ... how late we lost [baby] and how much of a person he is and was.</u> And I sometimes feel like when you ... they just go, "You had a stillborn", it just detracts every human part of that. And like, "Do you realise how developed he was? Do you realise how far along we were in this process? Do you realise, you know, that there are babies born 14 weeks before him and they survive and they're fine?" Like and that's not ... yeah we just kind of gloss over it as this term.' (Focus group participant; emphasis added)

(5.02) 'I agree with the terminology *full term stillbirth* because I think *stillbirth* is also used for late miscarriages sometimes too. And I think I agree <u>I want people to know that I carried my baby and I grew that baby until they were ready to be born.</u>' (Focus group participant; emphasis added)

As Middlemiss and Kilshaw's (2023) analysis highlights, however, the challenge with anything, including language, which seeks to validate feelings such as these is that it would simultaneously invalidate the experiences of others, many of whom already 'do experience hierarchies as social constraint, in some cases as disenfranchised grief' (p.15). Data extract 5.03 demonstrates this effect:

(5.03) 'I feel <u>quite sensitive about [*full term stillbirth*] being used, as in I want people to use [*stillbirth*] with [name]. She was on the earlier end, she was 25 weeks and five days</u> and not, admittedly, not medical professionals but other people I know have said that <u>it's not a birth, that she wasn't a person because it was so early.</u>' (Focus group participant; emphasis added)

In data extract 5.02, the participant objects to '*stillbirth* [being] also used for late miscarriages', whilst in 5.03, another participant refers to her daughter's gestational age at the time of her death as being 'on the earlier end'. Both quotations refer to the medico-legal dichotomy between miscarriage and stillbirth, sometimes referred to as the 'viability' threshold. In the UK, this threshold is 24 weeks; a *late miscarriage* is thus defined as the intrauterine death of a baby in the second trimester of pregnancy but before 24 weeks' gestation, whilst the 'earlier end' in 5.03 refers to the relative proximity of the baby's death to the 24-week threshold for stillbirth. These testimonies highlight not only the hierarchy perceived by some lived experience participants to exist within experiences of earlier and later stillbirth, but also that this hierarchy is mirrored and exaggerated in the distinction between miscarriage and stillbirth. In 5.02, this is expressed as a desire to use *full term stillbirth* to distinguish clearly between *late miscarriage* and the experience of stillbirth at an advanced stage of pregnancy. This reflects a broader tendency to equate younger gestational ages to lower psychological impact. In considering this tendency, Kraus (2022) argues that 'for physicians, the emotional impact of stillbirth tends to be experienced, and therefore perceived, as a much greater calamity' than losses earlier in pregnancy (p.238). As Kraus notes, this hierarchy of seriousness is effectively legitimised in many global territories by the dichotomy between miscarriage and stillbirth. After the 'viability' threshold, many legitimising rituals are facilitated, encouraged or even mandatory, such as 'memory-making' (Hennegan, Henderson, and Redshaw, 2015), photography (Oxlad *et al.*, 2023), parental leave, formal registration (Hodson, 2022), and holding a funeral. However, whilst usually technically possible following loss before a stillbirth threshold, be it 24 weeks, as in the UK, or otherwise, such rituals are often not facilitated or are even discouraged in cases of loss prior to the 'viability' threshold. In the case of parental leave, the 24-week stillbirth threshold has been described as an 'arbitrary cliff edge', creating a 'stark injustice' (Hodson, 2022).

In their consideration of US pregnancy loss terminology introduced in Section 2.1, clinicians Silver *et al.* (2011) likewise condemn the distinction in US law between pre- and post-20-week loss, miscarriage vs. stillbirth, as 'arbitrary', as well as scientifically 'unfounded' (p.1406). Silver *et al.* (2011) argue that 'the pathophysiologic events that precede births between 16 and 20 weeks are not significantly different from those preceding births after 20 weeks, manifested by cervical softening and effacement caused by infection or decidual hemorrhage or both' (pp.1406–1407), and that, on this basis, 'it makes no biological sense to draw an artificial line at 20 weeks of gestation. These births share pathophysiology and recurrence risk and should be described using similar terminology' (p.1407). Such arguments highlight the difficulty of disaggregating the need for legislative clarity, clinical and research precision, and cultural sensitivity.

In terms of cultural sensitivity, as was also discussed in Section 2, sociological research in the UK has shown that the dichotomisation of pre- and post-24-week loss, and the associated distinction between miscarriage and stillbirth, poses particularly acute challenges to those experiencing pregnancy loss between 20^{+0} and 23^{+6} weeks of pregnancy. Use of *miscarriage*, though reflective of the legislative and medical definition, can in such contexts be perceived as invalidating, as well as inadequately preparing families for the realities of labour and birth at such gestations (Smith *et al.*, 2020). As Smith *et al.* (2020) note, at such a gestation, 'the distinction between the terms 'miscarriage' and 'stillbirth' is not trivial. The term miscarriage focuses attention on the woman's body failing and denying fetal personhood' (p.872).

As Meluch (2022) notes in relation to pre-20-week pregnancy loss, 'when the way a traumatic diagnosis is communicated feels invalidating, it can make the entire medical experience feel undermined' (p.1453). In the specific context of the hinterland between legislative and medical definitions of miscarriage and stillbirth, terminology poses significant risks of this nature, and this is reflected in the testimonies of lived experience participants in this study who had experienced their loss(es) in the second trimester of pregnancy. All such participants strongly rejected the word *miscarriage* not just because of its perceived implication of blame, discussed in Subsection 4.1, but because it did not distinguish their experience from those occurring in the first trimester of pregnancy:

(5.04) 'I think the word *stillbirth* for the twins is the appropriate term ... <u>to call those babies at 22 and 23 weeks a *miscarriage* just seems completely ridiculous.</u>' (Focus group participant; emphasis added)

(5.05) 'I struggled with that, [with] *miscarriage* ... I didn't think that it described what I went through ... our baby that we met and saw. I don't think it described, and I'm not minimising miscarriage at all, because I know personally in my family, my sisters have been through miscarriages and <u>I'm not minimising at all. I just didn't think that *miscarriage* ... it was in between a *stillbirth* and *miscarriage* I felt</u> and so I like to refer to my loss as a *second trimester loss*.' (Focus group participant; emphasis added)

(5.06) '<u>The word *miscarriage*, I hate it.</u> [Name] was a baby. He was tiny, I held him in my hand, he had ten toes and ten fingers. Just gorgeous. But the *second trimester loss* sits better with me than a *miscarriage* like you said, <u>not downplaying it but that is not what happened to me in my head.</u>' (Focus group participant; emphasis added)

This distinction extended to situations where participants had experienced both first and second trimester losses. Here, several explicitly distinguished between the applicability of a word like *miscarriage* for their earlier and later experiences:

(5.07) 'I've now <u>had two actual miscarriages you know and it's really different</u> ... it's just not the same and to put that in the same category as delivering ... like, you know, going into hospital and delivering babies [at 17 weeks]. It's just ... it doesn't make any sense, [that] is on a completely different plane ... I guess what's important is ... you don't want to kind of come to a situation where people in first trimester miscarriages don't feel like that's taken seriously 'cause it's "only a miscarriage".' (Focus group participant; emphasis added)

In data extract 5.07, the participant distinguishes between what she considers to be 'actual miscarriages' occurring in the first trimester of pregnancy and 'going into hospital and delivering babies' at 17 weeks. Crucially, however, she recognises that the effect of making this comparison might be that 'people [experiencing] first trimester miscarriages don't feel like that's taken seriously'. As will be explored next, this is a pressing concern and one which relates directly to the so-called 'gender pain gap'. Others who compared personal experiences of losses in the first trimester and at later gestations stressed the physicality of the experience and the concrete separation from the baby who had died:

(5.08) 'Not to belittle anybody that's suffered miscarriages at all ... I mean I've had missed miscarriages, a 10 week [one], as well as ones at 8, 6, 7 weeks. But I think for me maybe because there's not a baby, a baby I can hold onto ... [the experience is less traumatic].' (Focus group participant)

Similarly, some participants compared their experiences of second trimester loss with the first trimester losses of others close to them:

(5.09) 'My friends have had different losses at different times, and none of them second trimester like mine. But certainly, [with] first [trimester loss], I think the difference is for them [they are] losing the future, losing the ... you know the thought of what you might have. Whereas I think, for me, the distinction in this case is losing something physical' (Focus group participant)

The distinction drawn in data extract 5.09 is between what psychotherapist Julia Bueno has categorised as the 'child in mind' (2019) and the physical experience of 'actually having to hold' a baby who has died, and 'having to leave [them] behind in the hospital'. While we must be extremely cautious of the risk of further disenfranchising the grief of those who experience types of pregnancy loss that do not involve this type of physicality, the physical experience of holding and leaving behind a baby was highlighted repeatedly as a cause of acute trauma in this project's dataset, and many reported that this trauma was exacerbated by language which they felt did not distinguish between experiences which are and are not physical in this way.

On the other hand, other personal accounts have highlighted that the 'absence of an embryo, of a *body*, can be particularly tormenting, as if it makes it a different, lesser category of miscarriage' (Agg, 2023, p.73), which further complicates the situation in relation to upholding this physical distinction.

Study participants who had lost babies in the second trimester overwhelmingly perceived it to be inaccurate and inappropriate to label their loss as *miscarriage*, feeling that this word fails to reflect the physicality of the experience and the gravity of what they had been through. This sense that the word *miscarriage* does not adequately reflect the gravity of the experience of losing a baby was also reflected in the testimonies of lived experience participants discussing first trimester loss, however:

(5.10) 'I feel like [*miscarriage*] downplays it, and I think lots of people think, "It's just an early miscarriage", or ... that many people have miscarriages, and I think people have that sort of mindset of, "Oh, at least it's early!" and that kind of thing ... I think that's my worry sometimes with *miscarriage*.' (Focus group participant; emphasis added)

Many participants who had lost a baby during the first trimester of pregnancy also explicitly rejected a hierarchical conceptualisation of loss which associates longer gestations with a higher level of grief or trauma:

(5.11) 'There is no hierarchy of grief. If you've lost a baby, you've lost a baby in my opinion ... nurses have said, "I had someone recently who was much further along than you", as if well I should be [thinking myself] lucky then, 'cause I'm 10 weeks and not 20 weeks. I think [people think] there's a hierarchy of loss.' (Focus group participant; emphasis added)

(5.12) 'I did find when people say, "Oh ... you miscarried", the first thing people say is, "How far gone were you?" It doesn't matter how far gone you were!' (Focus group participant; emphasis added)

In some cases, participants reported that the hierarchising impact of the 24-week stillbirth threshold had been made explicit in interactions with others. For the participant quoted in data extract 5.13, these interactions were in the context of employment, where she was given the impression that she was not entitled to use the word *stillbirth*:

(5.13) 'I chose [to use *stillbirth*] as well until I had people telling me it wasn't. [Name] was born um he may have been born sleeping but he was born; he was *stillborn* ... I emailed work saying, "This happened and I'm currently in hospital ... in a bereavement ward 'cause my baby is going to be born sleeping". And it was like, "Your baby is not a baby yet, it's not here yet so it's just a miscarriage".' (Focus group participant; emphasis added)

This kind of unofficial linguistic gatekeeping emphasises how pervasive hierarchical thinking around pregnancy loss is in UK society, as well as how closely tied it is to the 24-week legislative threshold. This has trickle-down effects on those who experience loss occurring at much younger gestational ages. It has been clear from this subsection that sharp divisions like those which exist in legislative and medical definitions in the UK and the United States do not always reflect the conceptual frameworks of those experiencing pregnancy loss. Kraus (2022) highlights the differences in the pregnancy loss narratives of healthcare professionals and those with lived experience; arguing for the importance of 'emphasising the value of even the earliest loss' in clinical practice (p.238). Agg (2023), however, notes that this is not usually how clinicians behave in reality, reflecting a 'hierarchy in terms of how healthcare professionals value miscarriages, devaluing losses that occur before a scan can be done' (p.182). Agg cites Professor Nick Macklon, who notes that:

> One of the reasons we assume women should handle a 'biochemical' pregnancy better than, say, a miscarriage after an early scan, is because of the importance that professionals place on saying, 'Look, I can see a foetal heart[beat]'. When that gets lost, it's no longer just an affair for the couple; other people have given it a certain value, which in a biochemical pregnancy hasn't happened yet. (quoted in Agg, 2023, p.182)

This, too, was reflected in participant testimonies collected during this study. Individuals who had experienced pregnancy loss in the first trimester clearly expressed a sense that their distress, grief, and trauma were frequently not acknowledged or understood by those involved in their care:

(5.14) 'I just thought there was no compassion, and it was very much a case of, "Well it's just a case of this, this is what it is". And even when it was a case of, "We're going to take the second fallopian tube," even then, "You're going to be infertile", there was no [cries] awareness of what that meant.' (Focus group participant; emphasis added)

A lack of research focusing on all aspects of female bodily experiences (Becher and Oertelt-Prigione, 2023; Sperber *et al.*, 2023) means that there is only a limited body of evidence considering the psychological impacts of first trimester pregnancy loss, whether independently or by comparison with other types of loss. What little data exist, however, indicate that the impacts of first trimester loss are extremely significant. Farren *et al.* (2016), for example, demonstrate high levels of Post Traumatic Stress Disorder following a loss during this trimester, whilst Hamama-Raz, Kraus, and Hamama (2024) have recently shown that the psychological sequelae of miscarriage and stillbirth (in this paper defined according to the Israeli threshold) were notably similar in many respects. The perceived lack of compassion highlighted in data extract 5.14 thus appears to persist despite a growing body of evidence indicating that compassion is no less called for in experiences of pregnancy loss in the first trimester than in later pregnancy. However, the participant data gathered during this study indicate that hierarchising conceptions of pregnancy loss are reflected in service provision around pregnancy loss in the UK. Many participants compared their experiences of pregnancy loss care and commented on the inconsistencies between NHS Trusts' and individual hospitals' policies and provision. For instance, in data extract 5.15, a participant who had lost her son in the second trimester of pregnancy recounts how she delivered her baby in a gynaecology ward and was made to feel unwelcome, as well as that staff 'didn't know what [they were] doing'. This extract is unusually long, because it provides context for the incident being reported.

(5.15) 'I was quite keen to know [where] you [other participants] delivered, in like what type of area in the hospital you delivered in? Because mine was in a [general] gynae[cology] ward and so it was full of ... older women and I was in a room [alone]. And then I was told by the doctor that "The nurses here are a bit pissed off that you're still here because we thought you'd be going in and out from surgery to do the cervical stitch," so that kind of put me on edge thinking, "Oh gosh, I hope I'm not disturbing these people who are obviously dealing with other things". And then I had nurses that were dealing with me and not an actual midwife that was there the whole time. And they did a couple of things which I can't ... I'm seeing a counsellor for. And I can't get out of my head the things that [they did], so I wonder [is] there a path[way] ... ? There should be a midwife that deals with this, who are trained [for it]. ... I'll explain some of the things that they did because this might help for us to somehow find a route where everyone's comfortable where they deliver ... within an hour or so I was I was delivering, and there was no [clinician] there. So we had to, obviously, call the bell to say, to tell the nurses to come in. And they were quite flustered ... And then I delivered ... I was sat on a commode and then I remember delivering and I said, "I need to wee," once I delivered I said, "Everything's out, I feel like everything's out," and <u>I said, "I need to wee". So obviously vocalised it without doing it and they said, "Yeah, just do it." So I actually weed on him and I didn't ... that [doesn't] really sit well with me because what I meant was for them ... I couldn't vocalise it [in] time [but] I needed them to remove the [baby]</u> ... And then even once we'd spent some time with [baby], one of the nurses came in [because] we pressed the bell and said that, you know, "We're ready for him to be taken now," and she came in, she looked at us and looked at him and walked straight back out, like she didn't know what she was doing. And after another 15 minutes I was saying to my husband, "I'm done with this, like, you know we've had our time and it's a lot of pain ... we've said our goodbyes now, so I called again and [another] nurse came and they kind of helped and kind of took him. But it just felt like no one knew what they were doing and when I did speak to, finally after a few <u>weeks I found the bereavement midwife, they basically said they don't take people [who have experienced loss at] under 20 weeks so they're not helping me.</u>'
(Focus group participant; emphasis added)

This participant reports that the sense that staff did not know how to facilitate her son's preterm delivery, and their consequent instruction that she should urinate on him once he had been delivered into a commode, has resulted in significant trauma, for which she has sought psychological support. This harrowing testimony highlights both discrepancies in pregnancy loss aftercare, since this participant has been told that in her NHS Trust bereavement midwives only support people experiencing loss after 20 weeks' gestation, and discrepancies in service provision during experiences of pregnancy loss. The other participants in the same focus group as the participant quoted in 5.15 had both had more positive experiences of delivery, despite delivering their babies at similar gestational ages:

(5.16) 'That makes me feel really lucky because we were in the [charity] Sands' bereavement delivery suite. [T]he hospital [we attended] has two rooms dedicated to Sands so we were really fortunate. We have two bereavement midwives and a midwife that was on duty with us.' (Focus group participant; emphasis added)

(5.17) 'They shouldn't have told me, but they were like "Well you can't use the bereavement suite because it's being refurbished". But, they put me ... on the [labour and] delivery suite down the end of the corridor, away from other people [giving birth], you know, and I had a choice of rooms ... I'm not sure how normal that is to be delivering elsewhere in the hospital because if something goes wrong like are those nurses trained in checking a placenta, etc.?' (Focus group participant; emphasis added)

These data extracts highlight the significant disparities in care experienced by participants going through pregnancy loss before 24 weeks, both during delivery and in terms of aftercare. Such disparities were also reflected in focus group data gathered during focus groups on first trimester pregnancy loss, with some participants in these groups reporting access to bereavement aftercare and others reporting no access to such provisions. Whilst not directly linguistic issues, these participants' experiences manifest the hierarchisation of pregnancy loss types, and this impact cannot be separated from language. The interconnected nature of hierarchical conceptions of pregnancy loss and language is most salient in relation to experiences such as that reflected in data extract 5.13, earlier, where the codification of a hierarchy in medico-legal definitions of miscarriage and stillbirth results in a graded model of care provision. However, given the apparent interdependency of terminology for pregnancy loss and cognitive conceptualisations of pregnancy loss, demonstrated earlier, it seems prudent to ask whether language such as *miscarriage* which is widely perceived in project data to 'downplay' experiences (extract 5.10) may play a role in upholding attitudes and practices like those described in data extract 5.15.

Whilst further research which considers this question is needed, it remains clear that despite recommendations aimed at promoting empathetic, patient-centred communication, and care more broadly, no matter the gestation at which a loss occurs (e.g., Kraus, 2022), healthcare professional participants do continue to feel that hierarchies of loss exist. This is reflected, for example, in data extract 5.18:

(5.18) 'In terms of like is there a hierarchy or not . . . I think we like to think there isn't but I think certainly when I've spoken to other clinicians there is [one] . . . "OK you've had a six week loss, really sorry about that", you know and the level of care that they can offer is quite different to a 22 week loss and the way we would talk about it I think changes, you know, that the . . . even just maybe subconsciously the way you think about it, the way I would, not care for that patient, but like the level of care you perhaps put out to that patient is different, the amount of time they might spend in the hospital would be different . . . I think there is, you know, it's quite a varied experience isn't it, in that . . . they're not having the same experience those two women, 6 weeks and then the 22 week loss.' (HCP focus group participant; emphasis added)

The persistent sense that experiences of pregnancy loss can be organised hierarchically, with stillbirths considered most traumatic and worthy of grief and first trimester losses least traumatic and worthy of grief would also seem to reflect the 'gender pain gap' (Guzikevits *et al.*, 2024; Patrick-Smith and Bull, 2024; Windrim, McGuire, and Durand, 2024), since they reflect a paternalistic perception that downplays experiences of first trimester pregnancy loss. The medical misogyny inherent in such perceptions of pregnancy loss, and the discourses and terminology associated with these perceptions, are the focus of the next subsection.

5.2 Medical Misogyny

In the previous section, many of the diagnostic labels used in connection with pregnancy loss were considered in terms of their fossilisation of attitudes towards pregnant bodies that are unacceptable in mainstream Western societies in the twenty-first century. The perception amongst lived experience study participants that diagnostic terms such as *miscarriage* and *incompetent cervix* imply responsibility and exacerbate self-reproach has been explored, as has the feeling amongst participants that words such as *termination* and *abortion* are associated not only with culpability but also with societal stigma. These perceptions were considered in the context of the social pressures placed on women and birthing people to fulfil the role of the 'good' mother (Miller, 2023, p.15) during pregnancy (Wolf, 2007). In the previous subsection, inconsistencies in the care received with losses occurring at different gestations during pregnancy were also considered, as potential corollaries of a hierarchising linguistic and conceptual taxonomy of pregnancy loss. In this subsection, these inconsistencies in care provision will be considered in more depth as a potential manifestation of medical misogyny. The focus here will be evidence, arising from lived experience study data, that pain and grief around pregnancy loss are sidelined, whilst birthing bodies are treated as problematic and deviant.

A growing body of evidence considers the 'gender pain gap' (Guzikevits *et al.*, 2024; Patrick-Smith and Bull, 2024; Windrim, McGuire, and Durand, 2024), one aspect of the gendered data gap known to exist both within and beyond medicine (Becher and Oertelt-Prigione, 2023; Sperber *et al.*, 2023). However, the notion that pain experienced and reported by those with bodies perceived to be female is taken less seriously than that of those with bodies perceived to be male is nothing new; the term 'Yentl syndrome' was coined (Healy, 1991) more than three decades ago, to describe the 'phenomenon of women's health symptoms being treated at lower rates than men's' (Guglielmo, 2018, 267). We now know that Yentl syndrome reflects a significant data gap, since most pharmaceutical trials are conducted on male bodies (Daitch *et al.*, 2022). We know, too, that women are more likely than men to experience more severe pain, but to wait longer for prescription of analgesics (Guzikevits *et al.*, 2024), and are more likely to be prescribed psychological treatments even where their incidence of depression is lower (Sundbom *et al.*, 2017).

Whilst women's health remains under-researched, all signs therefore point to systemic dismissal of female bodies' pain. Whilst medical misogyny also remains under-researched, there is therefore mounting evidence that those perceived to be women have their pain, both physical and psychological, ignored, downplayed, or distorted in clinical contexts, or have their bodies and minds represented as problematic or even broken when experiencing normal processes. Clement (2023) labels this phenomenon as 'medical gaslighting' and believes that it has 'links with misogyny' and 'with misogyny-affected individuals being less likely to be believed' (p.225), about their pain and other symptoms. Clement defines 'medical gaslighting' as 'healthcare concerns [being] dismissed or minimized to the point [the patient] question[s] their] reality' (Clement, 2023, p.225). There is ample evidence in the study data considered here that this medical gaslighting is normalised in contexts of pregnancy loss, and is often situated in terms of the 'normal' female bodily function of menstruation:

(5.19) 'I mentioned [my 6-week loss] to a family member [and] the response I got was, "Well, it's just a period". And that's a term that I've heard a lot and when I was going through my missed miscarriage, [a clinician] said, "When the bleeding starts <u>it's just gonna feel like a heavy period</u>".' (Focus group participant; emphasis added)

(5.20) '[I]t broke [my partner's] heart, hearing the word[s] "heavy period". Like, my partner is quite naïve in that situation because he's never gone through it. So because he was ... <u>taking the professional's word of just expecting me having a period</u> [the reality was a shock].' (Focus group participant; emphasis added)

Such experiences of a traumatic loss being minimised as 'just' a period highlight a dismissal of female pain strikingly reminiscent of Yentl syndrome. Similarly, the invalidation of feelings associated with pregnancy loss also seems to represent a form of medical gaslighting. In some cases, this gaslighting was associated with specific lexis, such as the diagnostic label *chemical pregnancy*. This label is used to describe a pregnancy loss occurring after pregnancy was confirmed using urine or blood testing, but before it can be located on an ultrasound.

(5.21) 'They used the language *chemical pregnancy* which was really difficult ... there was an undertone that it wasn't really real.' (Focus group participant)

(5.22) 'I hated the use of the word "chemical" ... which almost made the pregnancy feel like a figment of my imagination.' (Written contribution)

Similar sentiments were expressed in relation to *empty sac*, a diagnostic term which was also mentioned in Section 4. This phrase is used to describe the ultrasound finding in anembryonic pregnancies, when a baby stops developing before it can be seen on ultrasound, but the (apparently empty) gestational sac continues growing, with few or no outward signs of loss.

(5.23) '[*Empty sac*] is like the most horrible term because like then you think, "<u>Oh, is like, nothing even there?</u>"' (Focus group participant; emphasis added)

(5.24) '[*Empty sac*] sounds almost like it wasn't here ... [I]t just <u>makes you feel a bit crazy, almost, that you thought you were pregnant, you saw the tests, you get all the symptoms, and at that point it wasn't there.</u>' (Focus group participant; emphasis added)

(5.25) 'The [phrase] that they used was *empty sac* ... <u>like I imagined it in my head that we had the baby and that we fell pregnant</u>.' (Focus group participant; emphasis added)

By giving the impression that a pregnancy was a 'figment of the imagination', as noted in 5.22, *chemical pregnancy* and *empty sac* therefore appear to be associated with systemic misogyny of ignoring or minimising the pain of those assigned female at birth. In another apparent manifestation of medical gaslighting, other participants reflected on a perceived tendency to dismiss or minimise their experiences, with reference to those of others:

(5.26) 'One of the doctors ... was like, "You know, it's not a big deal. Some people are in here like 11 times!" and ... this was the consultant.' (Focus group participant)

(5.27) 'Being told by professionals it's common to have multiple miscarriages – it takes away from your experience.' (Written contribution)

Based on the dataset compiled in this study, this tendency to minimise experiences of pregnancy loss seems to be related primarily to first trimester pregnancy loss, despite such experiences being known to be associated with higher levels of PTSD than many modern wars (Farren *et al.*, 2016). Whilst this is, to some degree at least, a discursive feature which cannot be narrowed down to specific lexical items, several participants did implicate the word *miscarriage* in this systematic dismissal of the psychological suffering of those experiencing pregnancy loss before the 24-week UK threshold for categorising a stillbirth:

(5.28) 'I just worry people who haven't experienced it ... just think, "Oh, it's just like a female problem". Like, "It's just a miscarriage".' (Focus group participant)

(5.29) 'But that's what people imagine [when they hear *miscarriage*], "Oh you go to the toilet, you weed and there was some blood? I'm so sorry".' (Focus group participant)

On the other hand, contrary to this minimisation of loss as an expected 'female problem', some lived experience participants reported that they were made to feel that their bodies were 'broken' and abnormal. In the data for the study reported here, this was an impression associated especially with ectopic pregnancy, where an embryo implants somewhere other than the uterus, and which can cause life-threatening haemorrhage. Participants who had been through one or more ectopic pregnancy experiences reported feeling that their bodies were treated as deviant or aberrant:

(5.30) 'There was a lot of, "Oh, we're not seeing what we'd expect to see" or "There's nothing in the right place".' (Focus group participant)

(5.31) '[It] felt even more dehumanising, to keep hearing it being referred to as, "We don't even know where it is, we don't know where these cells are, we don't know where these tissues are". And it just made me feel very broken.' (Focus group participant; emphasis added)

(5.32) 'I found the ectopic the worst experience for sure, 'cause [I was made to feel] like a bit of an alien species really.' (Focus group participant; emphasis added)

The experiences highlighted in these data extracts, of being made to feel 'very broken' and 'like a bit of an alien species', reflect the discourses of abnormality accompanying less common experiences of pregnancy loss, like ectopic pregnancy. In some cases, as in data extract 5.33, these discourses of abnormality reflected clinicians' search for risk factors:

(5.33) 'I remember them saying to me, "You know, it's so rare to have two [ectopic pregnancies]". And it just made me feel like it was my fault even more. And it was like, "Oh, there must be something wrong with you, because this doesn't happen ... more than once," and "You know, it's really rare" ... Like, it didn't make me feel better that it was rare, it just made me feel worse. It made me feel even more like there was something wrong with me ... and there was loads of questions about, "Oh, are you sure you've never had an STI [Sexually Transmitted Infection], you sure you've never been diagnosed with endometriosis?". And I've never had an STI and I've never had ... investigations for endometriosis. And it's like, well there's nothing wrong with me so why has this happened? And why are you making me feel like it's my fault? Why are you making me feel like it must be something that I haven't told you? Because there's nothing.' (Focus group participant; emphasis added)

Here, the quoted participant reports insistent questioning about risk factors for ectopic pregnancy, including prior Sexually Transmitted Infection or endometriosis, and the impact of these discourses: 'it made me feel even more like there was something wrong with me'. In addition to relating back to the implication of culpability discussed in Section 4, these discourses also anticipate the discussion of risk communication in the next subsection.

5.3 Communicating about Risk

In concluding the previous subsection, data extract 5.33 highlighted the difficulty of being asked about prior Sexually Transmitted Infections and endometriosis in relation to her, rare, experience of recurrent ectopic pregnancy. For this participant, the clear implication behind these questions was that 'there was something wrong with me', and this was a sentiment likewise expressed by a number of other lived experience participants in relation to a variety of different types of pregnancy loss experience. Many participants reported feeling that their loss was being minimised when their age was mentioned as a risk factor:

(5.34) 'I just felt like such a number, and it didn't feel like my experience [mattered]. It just felt like I was a part of a pool of women, "It's very common," you know,

I'm nearly 40 so it's a case of, "You know, well [Participant], you know you are nearing that stage in life ... ". And it's like, "OK! We've got the age number. Like, you bring up age again and again. We shouldn't be talking about age when I've just gone through this like horrific, horrific experience!" (Focus group participant; emphasis added)

(5.35) I am 43 and they called me, "Of Advanced Maternal Age" ... Actually, I'm just a patient and just treat me like any other patient, don't treat me differently because I'm 43.' (Focus group participant; emphasis added)

The sense that care around traumatic experiences is being undermined by a preoccupation with age comes across in both data extracts 5.34 and 5.35. In 5.34, the participant says that they feel like 'a part of a pool of women', for whom pregnancy loss is 'very common' due to 'that stage in life', and in 5.35, the participant reports that she wishes not to be 'treat[ed] differently' due to age. Similar sentiments were expressed around weight, which participants felt was used to scapegoat them, or as a lazy excuse for not investigating causes of loss further:

(5.36) '[W]hen I was at my low point, I put on weight because I was comfort eating [after loss], and then obviously, I have seen the fertility consultant who mentioned weight ... For me when you're somebody who already [has] the guilt of, you know, losing your baby, to then be told "And now your weight". It's like another guilt thing.' (Focus group participant; emphasis added)

(5.37) '[S]ome of the language felt quite blameworthy which was difficult and upsetting. For example language around BMI, I always remember being told if you want fertility treatment on the NHS they won't look at you with BMI above 30 which was really upsetting, especially as testing after our losses revealed [the] cause was due to an autoimmune disorder ... so those many conversations around my weight felt quite unessacary [*sic*] considering auto-immune disorders were brushed over as being an unlikely cause of losses.' (Written contribution; emphasis added)

These testimonies highlight another gendered aspect of pregnancy loss experiences, since weight stigma is known to be a gendered issue in reproductive medicine (Evans and Vitek, 2023; Hill *et al.*, 2023) and beyond (Hatzenbuehler, Keyes, and Hasin, 2009). The tendency for 'fat women [to be] stigmatized more severely than men, and at lower weights' (Meadows *et al.*, 2022, p.36) is certainly reflected in the UK policy landscape around assisted conception, as well as participant data, with 'the vast majority of publicly subsidised IVF ha[ving] an absolute restriction to IVF access for any woman with a BMI over 30' (Mostaghim, 2024b), but few NHS Integrated Care Boards in the UK placing similar restrictions on partners of those seeking IVF, most of whom are male (Mostaghim, 2024a).

Testimonies quoted here in relation to age and weight stigma demonstrate that terminology and discourses around risk of pregnancy loss affect experiences of pregnancy loss. They also, moreover, indicate that these may be another manifestation of both the discourses of culpability for loss explored in Section 4 and of medical misogyny. As noted earlier, such medical misogyny means that women and other misogyny-affected individuals have their bodies and minds represented as problematic or even broken when experiencing normal processes. It is also notable that all data extracts quoted in this subsection relate to experiences of first trimester pregnancy loss. Overall, the study found that difficulties with pregnancy loss language were by no means confined to experiences of loss at earlier gestations, and this is reflected in other subsections as well as in Section 4. However, first trimester experiences predominate clearly in discussions of medical misogyny, and this indicates that this phenomenon may manifest to a greater extent in these contexts than when loss occurs in later pregnancy. This may relate to the perception that experiences of loss earlier in pregnancy are less traumatic and result in less grief, and therefore demand less sensitivity in communication, as was discussed in the previous subsection.

In the final section, the Element will conclude with a summary of the contributions it has made, and consideration of scope for future research.

6 Conclusion

> 'If the language isn't sensitive or considered, then it's just like a big fat arrow that says, "Yeah, you're to blame".'
> – Healthcare professional focus group participant, June 2024

This Element has explored the ways in which diagnostic terminology affects the experience of pregnancy loss in gendered ways. By examining participants' metalinguistic perceptions of pregnancy loss and the discursive representations of pregnancy loss associated with such terminology, the Element has highlighted both the key role language plays in healthcare around pregnancy loss and the gendered dimensions of the distress this language often causes. It has illuminated how diagnostic terms and the discursive practices surrounding them often reflect and perpetuate gendered expectations and societal norms, with significant psychological and emotional consequences for those affected.

The evidence presented in Section 4 highlights how specific terms, such as *miscarriage, pregnancy failure*, and *incompetent cervix*, are often perceived as loaded with implications of personal failure, culpability, and societal judgment. The metalinguistic contributions reveal that whilst some lived experience participants perceive these as external accusations, at a remove from their own bodily experience, others internalise them as judgments of their inability to fulfil the normative ideal of 'good motherhood' society imposes (Ellece, 2012; Coffey-Glover, 2020; Kinloch and Jaworska, 2021; Mackenzie, 2023). In this way, language plays an active role in constructing the emotional and psychological landscape of loss, framing it in ways that may deepen feelings of inadequacy and shame among women and other misogyny-affected groups. Similarly, as also explored in Section 4, use of terminology such as *termination* and *abortion* in the context of loss often intersects with deeply entrenched societal stigma surrounding reproductive rights and gendered expectations of motherhood (Mackenzie, 2018, 2023; Kinloch and Jaworska, 2021). The avoidance of such terms by some participants with lived experience of pregnancy loss underscores the extent to which lexical selection can perpetuate harmful stereotypes, reinforcing a dichotomy between 'acceptable' and 'unacceptable' forms of loss. The stigma associated with these terms reflects broader societal patterns of gendered behaviour policing, whereby women's reproductive experiences are frequently pathologised or moralised, and the dominant gendered discourses of good/bad motherhood explored in Section 1.3.

In Section 5, the discussion broadened to consider the systemic nature of the gendered discourses realised in pregnancy loss language (Sunderland, 2004). This section demonstrated that the impacts of pregnancy loss terminology extend beyond individual experiences of self-blame or shame; rather, these impacts reflect a healthcare system that often minimises, dismisses, or invalidates the pain of those who experience pregnancy loss. The gender pain gap, the tendency of healthcare institutions to dismiss or overlook pain and suffering expressed by women and other misogyny-affected groups, manifests in the discursive construction of pregnancy loss. Diagnostic terminology is thus, in this context, not merely a taxonomy of experiences but an active player in shaping the, often gendered, power dynamics between patients and healthcare professionals. The findings presented here therefore indicate that evidence-based reform of diagnostic terminology is not just a pressing need for improving communication but can also play a role in 'feminist analytical resistance', the first principle of Lazar's Feminist Critical Discourse Analysis (Lazar, 2005, p.5), by challenging wider issues of gender inequality within healthcare systems.

As was the case during the 'Death before Birth' project (Littlemore and Turner, 2019, 2020; Turner *et al.*, 2020; Austin *et al.*, 2021), the participatory model used to gather data for this Element has proven to be a valuable methodological approach in engaging with those who have lived experience of pregnancy loss. By centring their voices and experiences in the research process, this study provides a nuanced understanding of how individuals navigate the complex terrain of medical terminology, emotional pain, and social stigma. In doing so, it contributes to a more empathetic and informed discussion of pregnancy loss, one that is attuned to the ways in which language is both a source of harm and a potential source of healing.

The findings reported in this Element have implications for policy, clinical practice, and theory; both in the specific context of obstetric and gynaecological care and more broadly. A critical rethinking is needed, of the role that diagnostic terminology plays in shaping not only the emotional responses of those affected by experiences such as pregnancy loss but also the broader cultural and institutional frameworks within which those experiences are situated. The need for more precise, sensitive, and non-stigmatising language is evident, and recommendations based on the research reported here can be found elsewhere (Malory, 2024; Malory and Nuttall, 2024). However, it is also clear that linguistic reform cannot occur in isolation from broader structural changes. Language reform must be part of a larger effort to challenge the systemic inequities that characterise healthcare experiences for women and other misogyny-affected individuals.

Via its integrated focus on terminology and discourse, this Element not only represents a significant methodological departure from the existing body of research on pregnancy loss terminology but has also raised important questions about the intersection of language, gender, and clinical practice. By advocating for more thoughtful and inclusive linguistic practices, this work challenges us to reconsider how diagnostic terms and healthcare discourses can either reinforce or disrupt social inequalities. As research continues in this area, it is crucial to explore how linguistic changes might be implemented in practice, considering both the psychological needs of individuals and the sociocultural dynamics at play, as well as diverse settings such as clinical interactions and mass communication contexts. It is crucial that, as this project and its sister project have done, we continue to differentiate between language guidance appropriate to such distinct settings. This project has yielded recommendations (Malory, 2024) which acknowledge the significant variation in language needs amongst those with lived-body experience of pregnancy loss. These recommendations centre on guidance to actively elicit the preferences of those experiencing pregnancy loss, in order to respect the individual needs of service users in interpersonal clinical interactions, where this is feasible. Whilst these recommendations go beyond previous guidance for clinicians advising 'reflective listening' (Braillon and Taiebi, 2020), they do not make specific lexical prescriptions because, as the findings presented here show, diversity in the language needs of participants indicates that this would not be feasible. However, specific prescriptions are made by this study's sister project (Malory and Nuttall, 2024), which used a consensus model to identify least harmful terminology for pregnancy loss in mass communication contexts, where accommodating individual language needs is not feasible.

Future studies should examine the role of healthcare professionals in perpetuating or challenging these linguistic and discursive patterns, as well as the impact of cross-cultural differences in the language of pregnancy loss. They should also attempt to recruit more widely from the pool of potential participants affected by pregnancy loss. As noted in Section 3, given disproportionate rates of adverse pregnancy outcomes amongst Black and Asian ethnic groups (Knight *et al.*, 2023), recruitment efforts focused on attempting to ensure representation for these communities, but success in including racially minoritised participants was limited. This is reflected in the findings presented in this Element, which yield little insight into the different experience of minoritised groups. Future research should also seek to understand experiences of misogyny-affected individuals other than cisgender women, who made up the majority of the cohort for this study, as well as those of partners with experience of pregnancy loss that are not lived-body, including cisgender men.

In conclusion, the analysis presented in this Element highlights the need for ongoing critical engagement with the language of pregnancy loss and its broader implications. By acknowledging the gendered dimensions of diagnostic terminology and its impact on lived experience, this work calls for a more responsible, inclusive, and empathetic approach to both language and practice in the context of pregnancy loss. Only through such a multifaceted approach can we begin to address the emotional, psychological, and systemic inequities that continue to shape the experiences of those who face what is often a profound and traumatic loss.

References

Agatowski, T. (2023) 'The #RenamingRevolution Glossary is Here', 4 December. www.peanut-app.io/blog/renaming-revolution-glossary.

Agg, J. (2023) *Life, Almost: Miscarriage, Misconceptions and a Search for Answers from the Brink of Motherhood.* S.l. London: TORVA.

Andipatin, M. G., Naidoo, A. D., and Roomaney, R. (2019) 'The hegemonic role of biomedical discourses in the construction of pregnancy loss', *Women and Birth*, 32(6), pp. e552–e559. https://doi.org/10.1016/j.wombi.2019.03.006.

Austin, L., Littlemore, J., McGuinness, S., *et al.* (2021) 'Effective communication following pregnancy loss: A study in England', *Cambridge Quarterly of Healthcare Ethics*, 30(1), pp. 175–187. https://doi.org/10.1017/S0963180120000651.

Baker, M. R., Papp, L. J., Crawford, B. L., McClelland, S. I. (2023) 'Abortion stigma: Imagined consequences for people seeking abortion care in the United States', *Psychology of Women Quarterly*, 47(1), pp. 35–50. https://doi.org/10.1177/03616843221131544.

Bamber, A. R. (2022) 'Macerated stillbirth', in T. Y. Khong and R. D. G. Malcomson (eds.) *Keeling's Fetal and Neonatal Pathology.* Cham, Switzerland: Springer International, pp. 345–368.

Barad, K. (1998) 'Getting real: Technoscientific practices and the materialization of reality', *differences*, 10(2), pp. 87–128. https://doi.org/10.1215/10407391-10-2-87.

Baxter, J. (2003) *Positioning Gender in Discourse: A Feminist Methodology.* paperback ed. Basingstoke: Palgrave Macmillan.

BBC News (2022) 'Chrissy Teigen says she has come to realise she had an abortion, not a miscarriage', 16 September. www.bbc.co.uk/news/entertainment-arts-62925701#:~:text=%22It%20became%20very%20clear%20around,that%20had%20absolutely%20no%20chance%22.

Beard, R. W., Mowbray, J. F., and Pinker, G. D. (1985) 'Miscarriage or abortion', *Lancet (London, England)*, 2(8464), pp. 1122–1123. https://doi.org/10.1016/s0140-6736(85)90709-3.

Becher, E. and Oertelt-Prigione, S. (2023) 'The impact of sex and gender in medicine and pharmacology', in S. E. Tsirka and M. Acosta-Martinez (eds.) *Sex and Gender Effects in Pharmacology.* Cham: Springer International (Handbook of Experimental Pharmacology), pp. 3–23. https://doi.org/10.1007/164_2023_688.

Bird, F. (2020) 'A defense of objectivity in the social sciences, rightly understood', *Sustainability: Science, Practice and Policy*, 16(1), pp. 83–98. https://doi.org/10.1080/15487733.2020.1785679.

Bohren, M. A., Iyer, A., Barros, A. J. D., et al. (2024) 'Towards a better tomorrow: Addressing intersectional gender power relations to eradicate inequities in maternal health', *eClinicalMedicine*, 67, p. 102180. https://doi.org/10.1016/j.eclinm.2023.102180.

Braillon, A. and Taiebi, F. (2020) 'Practicing "reflective listening" is a mandatory prerequisite for empathy', *Patient Education and Counseling*, 103(9), pp. 1866–1867. https://doi.org/10.1016/j.pec.2020.03.024.

Brann, M., Bute, J. J., and Scott, S. F. (2020) 'Qualitative assessment of bad news delivery practices during miscarriage diagnosis', *Qualitative Health Research*, 30(2), pp. 258–267. https://doi.org/10.1177/1049732319874038.

Braun, V. and Clarke, V. (2021) *Thematic Analysis: A Practical Guide*. London: SAGE.

Brookes, G., Harvey, K., and Mullany, L. (2016) '"Off to the best start"?' *Gender and Language*, 10(3), pp. 340–363.

Bueno, J. (2019) *The Brink of Being: An Award-Winning Exploration of Miscarriage and Pregnancy Loss*. Hachette: Little, Brown Book Group.

Butler, J. (1990) *Gender Trouble*. London: Routledge.

Cameron, D. (1998) *The Feminist Critique of Language: A Reader*. Oxen: Routledge (World and Word Series). https://books.google.co.uk/books?id=4tAd-9g2bMkC.

Cameron, D. (2023) *Language, Sexism and Misogyny*. Oxen: Routledge.

Cameron, M. J. and Penney, G. C. (2005) 'Terminology in early pregnancy loss: What women hear and what clinicians write', *Journal of Family Planning and Reproductive Health Care*, 31(4), pp. 313–314. https://doi.org/10.1783/147118905774480761.

Chalmers, B. (1992) 'Terminology used in early pregnancy loss', *BJOG: An International Journal of Obstetrics & Gynaecology*, 99(5), pp. 357–358. https://doi.org/10.1111/j.1471-0528.1992.tb13746.x.

Chamberlain, G. (1997) 'Nomenclature: What is your name?' *BMJ*, 314(7095), pp. i–i. https://doi.org/10.1136/bmj.314.7095.0i.

Charmaz, K. (1983) 'The grounded theory method: An explication and interpretation', in R. M. Emerson (ed.) *Contemporary Field Research*. Boston: Little Brown, pp. 109–126.

Clement, C. (2023) *All Tangled Up in Autism and Chronic Illness: A Guide to Navigating Multiple Conditions*. London: Jessica Kingsley. https://books.google.co.uk/books?id=pCHZEAAAQBAJ.

Clement, E., Horvath, S., Koelper, N. C., & Sammel, M. (2017) 'The language of pregnancy demise: Patient-reported clarity and preferences', *Contraception*, 96(4), p. 300. https://doi.org/10.1016/j.contraception.2017.07.140.

Clement, E. G., Horvath, S., McAllister, A., *et al.* (2019) 'The language of first-trimester nonviable pregnancy: Patient-reported preferences and clarity', *Obstetrics & Gynecology*, 133(1), pp. 149–154. https://doi.org/10.1097/AOG.0000000000002997.

Coffey-Glover, L. (2020) 'The boob diaries: Discourses of breastfeeding in "exclusive pumping" blogs', *Discourse, Context & Media*, 38, p. 100446. https://doi.org/10.1016/j.dcm.2020.100446.

Cushing, I. and Snell, J. (2023) 'Prescriptivism in education', in J. C. Beal, M. Lukač, and R. Straaijer (eds.) *The Routledge Handbook of Linguistic Prescriptivism*. 1st ed. London: Routledge, pp. 194–212. https://doi.org/10.4324/9781003095125-14.

Daitch, V., Adi, T., Poran, I., *et al.* (2022) 'Underrepresentation of women in randomized controlled trials: A systematic review and meta-analysis', *Trials*, 23(1), p. 1038. https://doi.org/10.1186/s13063-022-07004-2.

Delabaere, A., Huchon, C., Lavoué, V., *et al.* (2014) 'Standardisation de la terminologie des pertes de grossesse : consensus d'experts du Collège national des gynécologues et obstétriciens français (CNGOF)', *Journal de Gynécologie Obstétrique et Biologie de la Reproduction*, 43(10), pp. 756–763. https://doi.org/10.1016/j.jgyn.2014.09.010.

Doka, K. J. (1999) 'Disenfranchised grief', *Bereavement Care*, 18(3), pp. 37–39. https://doi.org/10.1080/02682629908657467.

Edwards, E. (2012) *Foreword: Language, Prescriptivism, Nationalism – and Identity*. Berlin: De Gruyter Brill. https://doi.org/10.21832/9781847697813-004.

Eger, H. (2023) 'Health inequalities', in H. Eger (ed.) *Feminist Global Health Policy*. Wiesbaden: Springer Fachmedien Wiesbaden (BestMasters), pp. 5–25. https://doi.org/10.1007/978-3-658-43497-7_2.

Ehrlich, S. (2003) *Representing Rape: Language and Sexual Consent*. Oxon: Taylor & Francis. https://books.google.co.uk/books?id=vJCEAgAAQBAJ.

Ehrlich, S. (2009) 'Language, gender and sexuality', in K. Malmkjaer (ed.) *The Routledge Linguistics Encyclopedia*. Oxon: Taylor & Francis, pp. 308–316.

Ellece, S. E. (2012) 'The "placenta" of the nation', *Gender and Language*, 6(1), pp. 79–103. https://doi.org/10.1558/genl.v6i1.79.

Ellwood, D. A. and Flenady, V. (2019) 'Stillbirth', in S. Arulkumaran, W. Ledger, L. Denny, S. Doumouchtsis (eds.) *Oxford Textbook of Obstetrics and Gynaecology*. Oxford University Press (Oxford Textbook Series), pp. 422–434.

Evans, A. T. and Vitek, W. S. (2023) 'Weight bias in reproductive medicine: A curiously unexplored frontier', *Seminars in Reproductive Medicine*, 41(03/04), pp. 63–69. https://doi.org/10.1055/s-0043-1777016.

Fairclough, N. (1988) 'Discourse representation in media discourse', https://api.semanticscholar.org/CorpusID:147634980.

Farquharson, R. G., Jauniaux, E., and Exalto, N. (2005) 'Updated and revised nomenclature for description of early pregnancy events', *Human Reproduction*, 20(11), pp. 3008–3011. https://doi.org/10.1093/humrep/dei167.

Farren, J., M. Jalmbrant, L. Ameye, *et al.* (2016) 'Post-traumatic stress, anxiety and depression following miscarriage or ectopic pregnancy: A prospective cohort study', *BMJ Open*, 6(11), p. e011864. https://doi.org/10.1136/bmjopen-2016-011864.

Foucault, M. (1972) *Archaeology of Knowledge*. 1 ed. New York, NY: Routledge. https://doi.org/10.4324/9780203604168.

Gershenson, D. M., Valea, F. A., Lentz, G. M., Lobo, R. A. (2021) *Comprehensive Gynecology*. 8 ed. Philadelphia, PA: Elsevier. https://books.google.co.uk/books?id=20MCzgEACAAJ.

Gorfinkel, I. (2015) 'It's time to stop calling pregnancy loss "miscarriage"', *The Globe and Mail*, 15 October. www.theglobeandmail.com/life/health-and-fitness/health/its-time-to-stop-calling-pregnancy-loss-miscarriage/article26823539/.

Graumann, A. (2007) 'Color names and dynamic imagery', in M. Plümacher and P. Holz (eds.) *Speaking of Colors and Odors*. Amsterdam: John Benjamins. (Converging evidence in language and communication research), pp. 129–140.

Guglielmo, L. (2018) *Misogyny in American Culture: Causes, Trends, and Solutions [2 volumes]*. London: Bloomsbury.

Guzikevits, M., Gordon-Hecker, T., Rekhtman, D. *et al.* (2024) 'Sex bias in pain management decisions', *Proceedings of the National Academy of Sciences*, 121(33), p. e2401331121. https://doi.org/10.1073/pnas.2401331121.

Halliday, S., Romanis, E. C., de Proost, L., Verweij, E. J. (2023) 'The (mis)use of fetal viability as the determinant of non-criminal abortion in the Netherlands and England and Wales', *Medical Law Review*, 31(4), pp. 538–563. https://doi.org/10.1093/medlaw/fwad015.

Hamama-Raz, Y., Kraus, S., and Hamama, L. (2024) 'Experience of miscarriage versus stillbirth: Differences in fear of childbirth, adjustment disorder, and optimism', *Journal of Loss and Trauma*, 29(1), pp. 61–75. https://doi.org/10.1080/15325024.2023.2234822.

References

Hanschmidt, F., Linde, K., Hilbert, A., Riedel-Heller, S. G., Kersting, A. (2016) 'Abortion stigma: A systematic review', *Perspectives on Sexual and Reproductive Health*, 48(4), pp. 169–177. https://doi.org/10.1363/48e8516.

Hatzenbuehler, M. L., Keyes, K. M., and Hasin, D. S. (2009) 'Associations between perceived weight discrimination and the prevalence of psychiatric disorders in the general population', *Obesity*, 17(11), pp. 2033–2039. https://doi.org/10.1038/oby.2009.131.

Hays, S. (1996) *The Cultural Contradictions of Motherhood*. New Haven, CT: Yale University Press.

Healy, B. (1991) 'The Yentl Syndrome', *New England Journal of Medicine*, 325(4), pp. 274–276. https://doi.org/10.1056/NEJM199107253250408.

Hennegan, J. M., Henderson, J., and Redshaw, M. (2015) 'Contact with the baby following stillbirth and parental mental health and well-being: A systematic review', *BMJ Open*, 5(11), p. e008616. https://doi.org/10.1136/bmjopen-2015-008616.

Hill, B., Wynn-Jones, A. A., Botting, K. J. *et al.* (2023) 'The challenge of weight stigma for women in the preconception period: Workshop recommendations for action from the 5th European Conference on preconception health and care', *International Journal of Environmental Research and Public Health*, 20(22), p. 7034. https://doi.org/10.3390/ijerph20227034.

Hodson, N. (2022) 'Time to rethink miscarriage bereavement leave in the UK', *BMJ Sexual & Reproductive Health*, 48(1), pp. 70–71. https://doi.org/10.1136/bmjsrh-2021-201282.

Horstman, H. K., Holman, A., and McBride, M. C. (2020) 'Men's use of metaphors to make sense of their spouse's miscarriage: Expanding the communicated sense-making model', *Health Communication*, 35(5), pp. 538–547. https://doi.org/10.1080/10410236.2019.1570430.

Hutchon, D. J. R. (1998) 'Understanding miscarriage or insensitive abortion: Time for more defined terminology?' *American Journal of Obstetrics and Gynecology*, 179(2), pp. 397–398. https://doi.org/10.1016/S0002-9378(98)70370-9.

Johnson, B. L. and Quinlan, M. M. (2019) *You're Doing It Wrong!: Mothering, Media, and Medical Expertise*. New Brunswick, NJ: Rutgers University Press.

Johnson, J., Arezina, J., Hardicre, N. K. *et al.* (2020) 'UK consensus guidelines for the delivery of unexpected news in obstetric ultrasound: The ASCKS framework', *Ultrasound*, 28(4), pp. 235–245. https://doi.org/10.1177/1742271X20935911.

Kavanagh, Á. and Aiken, A. R. (2018) 'The language of abortion: Time to terminate TOP: FOR: Mandating TOP reduces research visibility and engenders stigma', *BJOG: An International Journal of Obstetrics & Gynaecology*, 125(9), pp. 1065–1065. https://doi.org/10.1111/1471-0528.15137.

Kinloch, K. and Jaworska, S. (2021) '"Your mind is part of your body": Negotiating the maternal body in online stories of postnatal depression on Mumsnet', *Discourse, Context & Media*, 39, p. 100456. https://doi.org/10.1016/j.dcm.2020.100456.

Klann, E. M. and Golabi, N. (2024) 'Abortion, reproductive justice, and intersectional inequity', in J. Bindeman (ed.) *The Mental Health Clinician's Handbook for Abortion Care*. Switzerland: Springer Nature, pp. 171–186.

Knaak, S. J. (2006) 'The problem with breastfeeding discourse', *Canadian Journal of Public Health*, 97(5), pp. 412–414. https://doi.org/10.1007/BF03405355.

Knight, M., Bunch, K., Felker, A. *et al.* (eds.) (2023) 'Saving Lives, Improving Mothers' Care Core Report – Lessons Learned to Inform Maternity Care from the UK and Ireland Confidential Enquiries into Maternal Deaths and Morbidity 2019–21.' National Perinatal Epidemiology Unit, University of Oxford. chrome-extension://efaidnbmnnnibpcajpcglclefindmkaj/https://www.npeu.ox.ac.uk/assets/downloads/mbrrace-uk/reports/maternal-report-2023/MBRRACE-UK_Maternal_Compiled_Report_2023.pdf.

Kolte, A. M., Bernardi, L. A., Christiansen, O. B. *et al.* (2015) 'Terminology for pregnancy loss prior to viability: A consensus statement from the ESHRE early pregnancy special interest group', *Human Reproduction*, 30(3), pp. 495–498. https://doi.org/10.1093/humrep/deu299.

Kraus, E. (2022) 'Humanizing the language and experience of pregnancy loss in health care', *Narrative Inquiry in Bioethics*, 12(3), pp. 235–240. https://doi.org/10.1353/nib.2022.0059.

Kumar, A., Hessini, L., and Mitchell, E. M. H. (2009) 'Conceptualising abortion stigma', *Culture, Health & Sexuality*, 11(6), pp. 625–639. https://doi.org/10.1080/13691050902842741.

Labov, W. (1994) *Principles of Linguistic Change. 1: Internal Factors*. repr. Chichester: Wiley-Blackwell (Language in society, 20).

Lacci-Reilly, K. R., Brunner Huber, L. R., Quinlan, M. M., Hutchison, C. B., Hopper, L. N. (2023) 'A review of miscarriage and healthcare communication in the United States', *Health Communication*, pp. 1–8. https://doi.org/10.1080/10410236.2023.2245205.

Lakoff, R. (1973) 'Language and woman's place', *Language in Society*, 2(1), pp. 45–80. www.jstor.org/stable/4166707?origin=JSTOR-pdf.

Lazar, M. M. (ed.) (2005) *Feminist Critical Discourse Analysis*. London: Palgrave Macmillan. https://doi.org/10.1057/9780230599901.

Lazar, M. M. (2007) 'Feminist critical discourse analysis: Articulating a feminist discourse Praxis1', *Critical Discourse Studies*, 4(2), pp. 141–164. https://doi.org/10.1080/17405900701464816.

Lindemann, K. (2018) 'Please, doctor, don't call my lost baby a "product of conception"', *The Guardian*, 8 November. www.theguardian.com/commentisfree/2018/oct/11/lost-baby-product-conception-grief-pregnancy-language.

Littlemore, J. and Turner, S. (2019) 'What can metaphor tell us about experiences of pregnancy loss and how are these experiences reflected in midwife practice?' *Frontiers in Communication*, 4. https://doi.org/10.3389/fcomm.2019.00042.

Littlemore, J. and Turner, S. (2020) 'Metaphors in communication about pregnancy loss', *Metaphor and the Social World*. John Benjamins, 10(1), pp. 45–75. https://doi.org/10.1075/msw.18030.lit.

Mackenzie, J. (2018) 'Good mums don't, apparently, wear make-up', *Gender and Language*, 12(1), pp. 114–135. https://doi.org/10.1558/genl.31062.

Mackenzie, J. (2019). *Language, Gender and Parenthood Online. Negotiating Motherhood in Mumsnet Talk*. London: Routledge. https://doi.org/10.4324/9781315146805.

Mackenzie, J. (2023) '"I had to work through what people would think of me": negotiating "problematic single motherhood" as a solo or single adoptive mum', *Critical Discourse Studies*, 20(1), pp. 88–105. https://doi.org/10.1080/17405904.2021.1997775.

Malory, B. (2022) 'The transition from *abortion* to *miscarriage* to describe early pregnancy loss in British medical journals: A prescribed or natural lexical change?' *Medical Humanities*, 48(4), pp. 489–496. https://doi.org/10.1136/medhum-2021-012373.

Malory, B. (2023) 'Polarized discourses of *abortion* in English: A corpus-based study of semantic prosody and discursive salience', *Applied Linguistics*, 45(3), p. amad042. https://doi.org/10.1093/applin/amad042.

Malory, B. (2024) 'Linguistic Challenges in Communicating about Pregnancy Loss: Final EStELC Project Report'. Survey of English Usage, University College London.

Malory, B. (2025) 'Language guidelines as the frontier of anti-prejudicial prescriptivism', in J. Setter, S. Dovchin, and V. Ramjattan (eds.) *Oxford Handbook of Language and Prejudice*. Oxford: Oxford University Press, pp. 623–643.

Malory, B. and Nuttall, L. (2024) 'Acceptability in pregnancy loss language'. Survey of English Usage, University College London. www.ucl.ac.uk/english-usage/staff/beth/resources/suppl-project-final-report.pdf (Accessed: 9 December 2024).

References

Martin, E. (2001) *The Woman in the Body: A Cultural Analysis of Reproduction.* Boston, MA: Beacon Press.

Martin, Z. (2023) '"The day joy was over:" Representation of pregnancy loss in the news', *Feminist Media Studies*, 23(5), pp. 2339–2354. https://doi.org/10.1080/14680777.2022.2051060.

Matley, D. (2020) '"I miss my old life": Regretting motherhood on Mumsnet', *Discourse, Context & Media*, 37, p. 100417. https://doi.org/10.1016/j.dcm.2020.100417.

Meadows, A., Daníelsdóttir, S., Goldberg, D., Mercedes, M. (2022) 'Fighting for a (wide enough) seat at the table: Weight stigma in law and policy', in S. von Liebenstein (ed.) *Legislating Fatness: Current Debates in Weight Discrimination, Policy, and Law.* Taylor & Francis, pp. 25–48. https://books.google.co.uk/books?id=9-pvEAAAQBAJ.

Meluch, A. L. (2022) 'Waiting to be seen: Provider-patient communication in the emergency room about miscarriage', *Health Communication*, 37(11), pp. 1452–1454. https://doi.org/10.1080/10410236.2021.1901421.

Middlemiss, A. L. and Kilshaw, S. (2023) 'Further hierarchies of loss: Tracking relationality in pregnancy loss experiences', *OMEGA – Journal of Death and Dying*, p. 003022282311822. https://doi.org/10.1177/00302228231182273.

Miller, T. (2023) *Motherhood: Contemporary Transitions and Generational Change.* Cambridge: Cambridge University Press.

Milroy, J. and Milroy, L. (2012) *Authority in Language: Investigating Standard English.* Oxon: Routledge (Routledge linguistics classics).

Mobbs, N., Williams, C., and Weeks, A. (2018) 'Humanising birth: Does the language we use matter?' *The BMJ Opinion*, 8 February. https://blogs.bmj.com/bmj/2018/02/08/humanising-birth-does-the-language-we-use-matter/.

Moore, J. and Abetz, J. S. (2019) 'What do parents regret about having children? communicating regrets online', *Journal of Family Issues*, 40(3), pp. 390–412. https://doi.org/10.1177/0192513X18811388.

Moscrop, A. (2013) '"Miscarriage or abortion?" Understanding the medical language of pregnancy loss in Britain; a historical perspective', *Medical Humanities*, 39(2), pp. 98–104. https://doi.org/10.1136/medhum-2012-010284.

Mostaghim, M. (2024a) '"(Re)producing evidence used to support funding exclusions for fat patients that seek in vitro fertilisation in NHS England."' *Broadly Conceived Conference 2024*, Birkbeck College, University of London.

Mostaghim, M. (2024b) 'Why is IVF access in the UK almost impossible with a high BMI?', *Big Birthas*. www.bigbirthas.co.uk/ivf-access-in-the-uk-impossible-with-a-high-bmi/ (Accessed: 23 December 2024).

Murkoff, H. (2018) *What to Expect When You're Expecting: 5th Edition of the World's Bestselling Pregnancy Book*. New York, NY: HarperCollins.

Murphy, E. (1999) '"Breast Is best": Infant feeding decisions and maternal deviance', *Sociology of Health & Illness*, 21(2), pp. 187–208. https://doi.org/10.1111/1467-9566.00149.

Murphy, E. (2000) 'Risk, responsibility, and rhetoric in infant feeding', *Journal of Contemporary Ethnography*, 29(3), pp. 291–325. https://doi.org/10.1177/089124100129023927.

Oré, M. (2020) 'Women are calling for the word miscarriage to be banished For good', *Glamour*, 10 January. www.glamour.com/story/women-are-calling-for-the-word-miscarriage-to-be-banished-for-good (Accessed: 22 November 2023).

Oxlad, M. J., Franke, E. F., Due, C., Jaensch, L. H. (2023) 'Capturing parents' and health professionals' experiences of stillbirth bereavement photography: A systematic review and meta-synthesis', *Women and Birth*, 36(5), pp. 421–428. https://doi.org/10.1016/j.wombi.2023.03.001.

Papen, U., Peach, E., Casaponsa, A., Atanasova, D. (2022) 'Research ethics in (applied) linguistics', in J. Culpeper *et al.* (eds.) *Introducing Linguistics*. Oxon: Routledge (Learning about language), pp. 355–367.

Patrick-Smith, M. and Bull, S. (2024) 'Medical student perceptions of gender and pain: A systematic review of the literature', *BMC Medicine*, 22(1), p. 434. https://doi.org/10.1186/s12916-024-03660-0.

Peanut (2023) 'Renaming revolution: The motherhood and fertility glossary'. *Peanut*. www.peanut-app.io/blog/renaming-revolution-glossary.

Percy, C. and Davidson, M. C. (2012) *The Languages of Nation*. Bristol: Channel View (Multilingual Matters). https://books.google.co.uk/books?id=7zdqxQ-ktAwC.

Pinar, M. H., Gibbins, K., He, M., Kostadinov, S., Silver, R. (2018) 'Early pregnancy losses: Review of nomenclature, histopathology, and possible etiologies', *Fetal and Pediatric Pathology*, 37(3), pp. 191–209. https://doi.org/10.1080/15513815.2018.1455775.

Pütz, M. and Verspoor, M. (2000) 'Introduction', in M. Pütz and M. Verspoor (eds.) *Explorations in Linguistic Relativity*. Amsterdam: J. Benjamins (4]), pp. ix–xvi.

Reed, K., Ellis, J., and Whitby, E. (2023) *Understanding Baby Loss: The Sociology of Life, Death and Post-Mortem*. Manchester: Manchester University Press. https://books.google.co.uk/books?id=DSTuEAAAQBAJ.

Robson, P. and Walter, T. (2013) 'Hierarchies of loss: A critique of disenfranchised grief', *OMEGA – Journal of Death and Dying*, 66(2), pp. 97–119. https://doi.org/10.2190/OM.66.2.a.

References

Royal College of Midwives (2022) 'The Re:Birth Project, Final Report'. Royal College of Midwives. chrome-extension://efaidnbmnnnibpcajpcglclefindmkaj/https://www.rcm.org.uk/media/6327/rebirth-final-full-report-july-2022.pdf.

Royal College of Obstetricians and Gynaecologists (2022) 'RCOG Language Guide'. Royal College of Obstetricians and Gynaecologists.

Russo, N. F. (1976) 'The motherhood mandate', *Journal of Social Issues*, 32(3), pp. 143–153. https://doi.org/10.1111/j.1540-4560.1976.tb02603.x.

Sekalala, S. and Niezgoda, B. C. (2018) *Global Perspectives on Health Communication in the Age of Social Media*. IGI Global (Advances in Healthcare Information Systems and Administration (2328–1243)).

Silver, R. M., Branch, D. W., Goldenberg, R., Iams, J. D., Klebanoff, M. A. (2011) 'Nomenclature for pregnancy outcomes: Time for a change', *Obstetrics & Gynecology*, 118(6), pp. 1402–1408. https://doi.org/10.1097/AOG.0b013e3182392977.

Smith, L., Dickens, J., Atik, R. B. *et al.* (2020) 'Parents' experiences of care following the loss of a baby at the margins between miscarriage, stillbirth and neonatal death: A UK qualitative study', *BJOG: An International Journal of Obstetrics & Gynaecology*, 127(7), pp. 868–874. https://doi.org/10.1111/1471-0528.16113.

Spender, D. (1998) *Man Made Language*. Oxon: Pandora.

Sperber, S., Täuber, S., Post, C., Barzantny, C. (2023) 'Gender data gap and its impact on management science – Reflections from a European perspective', *European Management Journal*, 41(1), pp. 2–8. https://doi.org/10.1016/j.emj.2022.11.006.

Steer, P. J. (2018) 'The language of abortion: Time to terminate TOP: AGAINST: "Termination of pregnancy" is less likely than "abortion" to be misunderstood or cause distress', *BJOG: An International Journal of Obstetrics & Gynaecology*, 125(9), pp. 1066–1066. https://doi.org/10.1111/1471-0528.15136.

Sundbom, L. T., Bingefors, K., Hedborg, K., Isacson, D. (2017) 'Are men under-treated and women over-treated with antidepressants? Findings from a cross-sectional survey in Sweden', *BJPsych Bulletin*, 41(3), pp. 145–150. https://doi.org/10.1192/pb.bp.116.054270.

Sunderland, J. (2000) 'Baby entertainer, bumbling assistant and line manager: Discourses of fatherhood in parentcraft texts', *Discourse & Society*, 11(2), pp. 249–274. https://doi.org/10.1177/0957926500011002006.

Sunderland, J. (2004) *Gendered Discourses*. London: Palgrave Macmillan. https://doi.org/10.1057/9780230505582.

Sunderland, J. (2012) *Language, Gender and Children's Fiction*. London: Continuum Logo.

Talbot, J. (2018) 'Flat ontologies and everyday feminisms: Revisiting personhood and fetal ultrasound', in J. Jung and A. Booher (eds.) *Feminist Rhetorical Science Studies: Human Bodies, Posthumanist Worlds*. Carbondale, IL: Southern Illinois University Press (Studies in Rhetorics and Feminisms), pp. 84–113.

Tommy's (no date) 'Miscarriage stigma as a British Indian family', *Tommy's Baby Loss Stories*. www.tommys.org/baby-loss-support/baby-loss-stories/miscarriage-stigma-british-indian-family.

Turner, S., Littlemore, J., Fuller, D., Kuberska, K., McGuinness, S. (2020) 'The production of time-related metaphors by people who have experienced pregnancy loss', in J. Barnden and A. Gargett (eds.) *Figurative Thought and Language*. Amsterdam: John Benjamins, pp. 389–418. https://doi.org/10.1075/ftl.10.14tur.

Valentine, D. P. (2019) *Infertility and Adoption: A Guide for Social Work Practice*. Oxon: Taylor & Francis. https://books.google.co.uk/books?id=85SpDwAAQBAJ.

Vimalesvaran, S., Ireland, J., and Khashu, M. (2021) 'Mind your language: Respectful language within maternity services', *The Lancet*, 397(10277), pp. 859–861. https://doi.org/10.1016/S0140-6736(21)00031-3.

Weedon, C. (1997) *Feminist Practice & Poststructuralist Theory*. 2nd ed. Oxford: Blackwell.

Windrim, E. B., McGuire, B. E., and Durand, H. (2024) 'Women's experiences of seeking healthcare for abdominal pain in Ireland: A qualitative study', *BMC Women's Health*, 24(1), p. 166. https://doi.org/10.1186/s12905-024-02995-3.

Wolf, J. B. (2007) 'Is breast really best? risk and total motherhood in the national breastfeeding awareness campaign', *Journal of Health Politics, Policy and Law*, 32(4), pp. 595–636. https://doi.org/10.1215/03616878-2007-018.

Wolf, J. B. (2010) *Is Breast Best?: Taking on the Breastfeeding Experts and the New High Stakes of Motherhood*. New York: NYU Press.

Wolfram, W. and Schilling, N. (2015) *American English: Dialects and Variation*. Hoboken, NJ: Wiley (Language in Society). https://books.google.co.uk/books?id=vPdgBgAAQBAJ.

Yip, J. L. Y., Poduval, S., de Souza-Thomas, L., Carter, S., Fenton, K. (2024) 'Anti-racist interventions to reduce ethnic disparities in healthcare in the UK: An umbrella review and findings from healthcare, education and criminal justice', *BMJ Open*, 14(2), p. e075711. https://doi.org/10.1136/bmjopen-2023-075711.

Acknowledgments

I am deeply indebted to the participants of the EStELC project, without whom this Element would not exist. I hope it does justice to your experiences and your babies. I am grateful, too, to the EStELC Expert Advisory Group for their invaluable input throughout the project.

I am also indebted to the anonymous reviewers who commented on a draft version of this Element. These comments and suggestions were invaluable and have improved the Element immeasurably.

This work was supported by the Arts and Humanities Research Council (grant number AH/X003973/1). Funding from AHRC also made it possible for this book to be published open access, making the digital version freely available for anyone to read and reuse under a Creative Commons licence.

Cambridge Elements

Language, Gender and Sexuality

Helen Sauntson
York St John University

Helen Sauntson is Professor of English Language and Linguistics at York St John University, UK. Her research areas are language in education and language, gender and sexuality. She is co-editor of *The Palgrave Studies in Language, Gender and Sexuality* book series, and she sits on the editorial boards of the journals *Gender and Language* and the *Journal of Language and Sexuality*. Within her institution, Helen is Director of the Centre for Language and Social Justice Research.

Holly R. Cashman
University of New Hampshire

Holly R. Cashman is Professor of Spanish at University of New Hampshire (USA), core faculty in Women's and Gender Studies, and coordinator of Queer Studies. She is past president of the International Gender and Language Association (IGALA) and of the executive board of the Association of Language Departments (ALD) of the Modern Languages Association. Her research interests include queer(ing) multilingualism and language, gender, and sexuality.

Editorial Board
Lilian Lem Atanga, *The University of Bamenda*
Eva Nossem, *Saarland University*
Joshua M. Paiz, *The George Washington University*
M. Agnes Kang, *University of Hong Kong*

About the Series
Cambridge Elements in Language, Gender and Sexuality highlights the role of language in understanding issues, identities and relationships in relation to multiple genders and sexualities. The series provides a comprehensive home for key topics in the field which readers can consult for up-to-date coverage and the latest developments.

Cambridge Elements

Language, Gender and Sexuality

Elements in the Series

The Language of Gender-Based Separatism
Veronika Koller, Alexandra Krendel and Jessica Aiston

Queering Sexual Health Translation Pedagogy
Piero Toto

Legal Categorization of "Transgender": An Analysis of Statutory Interpretation of "Sex", "Man", and "Woman" in Transgender Jurisprudence
Kimberly Tao

LGBTQ+ and Feminist Digital Activism: A Linguistic Perspective
Angela Zottola

Feminism, Corpus-assisted Research and Language Inclusivity
Federica Formato

Queering Language Revitalisation: Navigating Identity and Inclusion among Queer Speakers of Minority Languages
John Walsh, Michael Hornsby, Eva J. Daussà, Renée Pera-Ros, Samuel Parker, Jonathan Morris and Holly R. Cashman

Pride in Asia: Negotiating Ideologies, Localness, and Alternative Futures
Benedict J. L. Rowlett, Pavadee Saisuwan, Christian Go,
Li-Chi Chen and Mie Hiramoto

Language, Gender, and Pregnancy Loss
Beth Malory

A full series listing is available at: www.cambridge.org/ELGS

Printed by Integrated Books International,
United States of America